Management Extra

REACHING YOUR GOALS THROUGH INNOVATION

Management Extra

REACHING YOUR GOALS THROUGH INNOVATION

AMSTERDAM • BOSTON • HEIDELBERG • LONDON • NEW YORK • OXFORD • PARIS •
SAN DIEGO • SAN FRANCISCO • SINGAPORE • SYDNEY • TOKYO

Pergamon Flexible Learning is an imprint of Elsevier
Linacre House, Jordan Hill, Oxford OX2 8DP, UK
30 Corporate Drive, Suite 400, Burlington, MA 01803, USA

First edition 2007

British Library Cataloguing in Publication Data
A catalogue record for this book is available from the British Library

Library of Congress Cataloging-in-Publication Data
A catalog record for this book is available from the Library of Congress

ISBN–13: 978-0-08-046527-2
ISBN–10: 0-08-046527-7

For information on all Pergamon Flexible Learning publications visit our web site at books.elsevier.com

Printed and bound in Italy

07 08 09 10 11 10 9 8 7 6 5 4 3 2 1

Contents

Contents

Activities

Figures

Tables

Series preface

Whether you are a tutor/trainer or studying management development to further your career, Management Extra provides an exciting and flexible resource helping you to achieve your goals. The series is completely new and up-to-date, and has been written to harmonise with the 2004 national occupational standards in management and leadership. It has also been mapped to management qualifications, including the Institute of Leadership & Management's middle and senior management qualifications at Levels 5 and 7 respectively on the revised national framework.

For learners, coping with all the pressures of today's world, Management Extra offers you the flexibility to study at your own pace to fit around your professional and other commitments. Suddenly, you don't need a PC or to attend classes at a specific time – choose when and where to study to suit yourself! And, you will always have the complete workbook as a quick reference just when you need it.

For tutors/trainers, Management Extra provides an invaluable guide to what needs to be covered, and in what depth. It also allows learners who miss occasional sessions to 'catch up' by dipping into the series.

This series provides unrivalled support for all those involved in management development at middle and senior levels.

Reviews of Management Extra

> *I have utilised the Management Extra series for a number of Institute of Leadership and Management (ILM) Diploma in Management programmes. The series provides course tutors with the flexibility to run programmes in a variety of formats, from fully facilitated, using a choice of the titles as supporting information, to a tutorial based programme, where the complete series is provided for home study. These options also give course participants the flexibility to study in a manner which suits their personal circumstances. The content is interesting, thought provoking and up-to-date, and, as such, I would highly recommend the use of this series to suit a variety of individual and business needs.*

Martin Davies BSc(Hons) MEd CEngMIMechE MCIPD FITOL FInstLM
Senior Lecturer, University of Wolverhampton Business School

> *At last, the complete set of books that make it all so clear and easy to follow for tutor and student. A must for all those taking middle/senior management training seriously.*

Michael Crothers, ILM National Manager

'Chance favours only the prepared mind'

Louis Pasteur

Successful innovation isn't about being lucky. It may have looked like Pasteur hit the jackpot when he discovered the germ theory of disease, but it wasn't by chance. Far from it. Whilst not necessarily by design, the whole process of discovery, from bacteria in wine to immunisation theory was about being prepared to find and see the right answers.

This book explores the concept of spotting good ideas, linking them to the business context and making them work. In doing so you will be reaching, achieving and even exceeding your goals.

Good ideas

To start the journey you need to know where you are heading; which direction will take you where you need to go. If you know where you are going, how will you bring your team along too and what improvements can you make to the way you work together. This book looks at the role of a manager in the process of target setting and innovation. The role is intended in its broadest sense to encompass people with responsibility for project teams and external teams and well as internal teams.

Change is the law of life. And those who look only to the past or present are certain to miss the future.

John F. Kennedy

Organisations are not straightforward. You're almost bound to go off course. You'll be buffeted by new ideas, change or new people all of which can take you in a different direction. How do you recognise which avenues to follow and which to leave well alone?

The themes of this book reflect the dichotomy of Pasteur's series of apparent chance discoveries against his preparedness. It's about the need to know your course and what you are trying to achieve, without being blinkered to the potential for improvement. In other words being able to see, evaluate and grasp opportunities as they arise.

Your objectives are to:

- use objectives and goals to help you set direction and monitor outcomes for you and your team
- review the organisational context for innovation and how to make things happen
- understand the characteristics of successful innovators and your role in championing opportunities for innovation

- evaluate potential quality improvements that can be made
- identify opportunities for innovation and encourage creativity
- understand the risks and benefits, feasibility and viability of new ideas.

1 Setting your direction

Making objectives and targets work for you

Why are objectives and targets so important? The answer lies in what they can do for you.

- Objectives tell you where you need to go.
- Objectives are specific.
- Objectives are normally manageable components of a wider aim.
- Objectives tell you when and what needs to be achieved – the standards of service required.

- Targets define the end game in terms of numbers or finances.
- Targets are motivational.
- Targets make it clear to people how much they are contributing.
- Targets can be broken down into manageable chunks.

Meeting your objectives and targets will enable you to know when you've achieved something.

This theme looks at the role of objectives and targets in helping you as an individual and as a leader, to communicate, negotiate with and influence the people you work with to achieve your goals. The strategic importance of this is measurable in terms of meeting what is expected of you and vital in terms of your relationship with your team and their motivation to achieve for themselves, for you and for the organisation.

In this theme you will:

- **use objectives and targets to help set direction for you and your team**
- **negotiate objectives to meet organisational needs**
- **understand how delegation will help you and your team achieve objectives**
- **monitor the outcomes.**

On course

People will only follow if the manager or leader creates a clear vision. As a leader you have to be able to answer the questions:

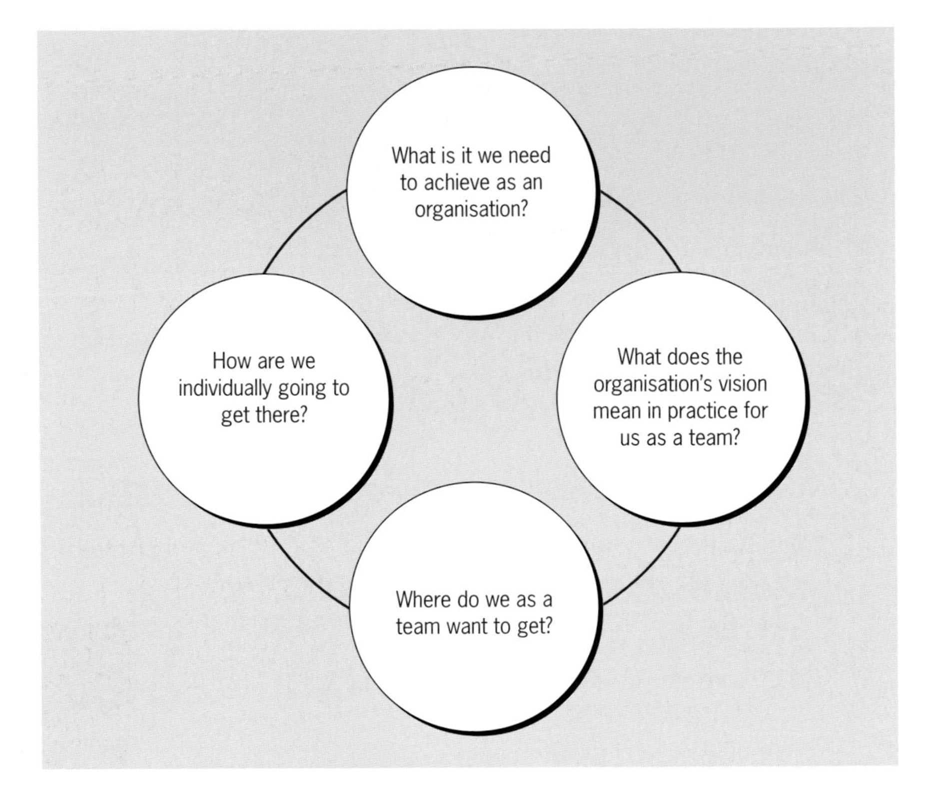

Figure 1.1 *Setting your direction*

It's worth taking the opportunity to involve your team in answering these questions. The more they're involved; the greater their sense of ownership and commitment will be.

John Adair describes leadership in the following way.

> 'Leadership involves focusing the efforts of a group of people towards a common goal and enabling them to work together as a team.'

It's essentially about pulling in the same direction. Every single team member's individual objectives must ultimately contribute to the organisational goals. In other words, aligning the business.

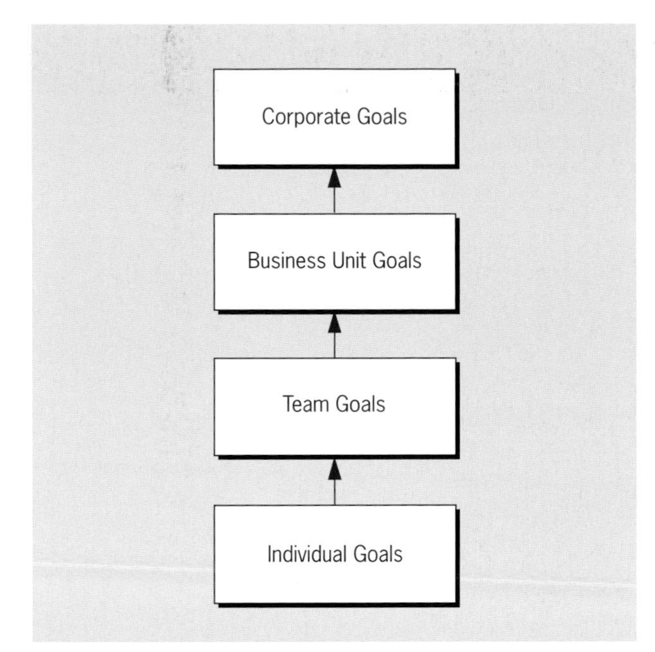

Figure 1.2 *Aligning goals*

This involves cascading objectives down the organisation or up from the individual. From individual targets and objectives to team, to organisational objectives. Individuals should be able to clearly see how they are doing their bit towards the organisational vision.

Your role is to make sure that the objectives of every member of your team align to the team or project objectives. You'll also need to be sure that the team objectives fit neatly into the bigger departmental and organisational picture. If they don't fit, they aren't worth doing.

'There is nothing so useless as doing efficiently that which should not be done at all.'
Peter Drucker

Defining organisational vision and direction

An organisation's vision is unique and represents the time, place and business environment in which it operates.

Here are two examples of organisations at either end of a strategic dynamic scale. It is a scale that will have a significant impact on the vision and direction of the organisation.

Organisation 1 is faced with rapid changes in:

- technology, consumer behaviour and social values
- customers bringing new ideas as a spark for growth
- financial returns from a product nearing the end of its life cycle.

In contrast, Organisation 2 takes a longer term approach when:

- it operates as a public service organisation with commitments to transferred employees
- the existing culture is to reward safe policies that achieve stated targets
- new opportunities are measured against prevailing public perceptions.

Their strategic direction might look something like this.

Organisation 1 will need to:

- focus on action
- take decisions within a short time-scale
- manage resources so that they can be committed (or withdrawn) rapidly
- clearly define areas of responsibility for decision making.

Organisation 2 on the other hand, is more likely to find:

- decision-making involves committees and larger numbers of people
- decisions are based on compromise, encouraging slower paced change
- the focus is on minimising exposure to risk.

The vision is a clear statement which expresses the organisation's aims, and often, where it lies on that continuum between dynamic, leaders in the field, who innovate, but expose themselves to risk; and low risk, considered organisations that protect employees from rapid upheaval. The vision also tends to express some of the key things that the organisation values, such as respect, integrity, sustainability and customer focus. Values set the context for the way people in the organisation behave and what is expected of them.

Here are some examples of vision statements.

At Sainsbury's we will deliver an ever improving quality shopping experience for our customers with great product at fair prices. We aim to exceed customer expectations for healthy, safe, fresh and tasty food making their lives easier every day.

Source: Sainsbury Web site

Sainsbury's clearly state their desire to be a fair and forward thinking organisation that is looking to move in ways that their customers value. Their vision is one that attempts to appeal to the values of their customers. We will of course form our own views on whether they are able to achieve this in practice.

> We believe in making a difference. In our customers' eyes, Virgin stands for value for money, quality, innovation, fun and a sense of competitive challenge. We deliver a quality service by empowering our employees and we facilitate and monitor customer feedback to continually improve the customer's experience through innovation.

www.virgin.com

Virgin on the other hand takes the perspective of the customer including elements of fun and challenge and customer feedback. They also focus on employees and they way they work in their vision.

> After a year of debate and consultation, our staff and students have articulated a proud ambition and sense of purpose – to work and study in a world-class university which makes a difference. To achieve this, the University has launched a new strategy with a map to help us get there.

www.leeds.ac.uk

Leeds University has proudly articulated its mission to make a difference. They highlight the consensual and co-operative development of the mission, thereby expressing the commitment to hearing and valuing the views of all stakeholders.

These are just the headline statements, but even as headlines they start to define the direction and some of the values underpinning the organisations they represent.

Translating the vision and values into objectives

The organisational vision has two primary roles. To set direction for employees and stakeholders and to help the organisation express what it values to the wider world.

The process of translating the vision into objectives is normally the remit of managers within the organisation. Most strategies set out what needs to be achieved and the level of innovation desired and this can be broken down into areas, divisions and team targets. The process of setting objectives at every level needs to be aligned to ensure the overall goals of the organisation are met.

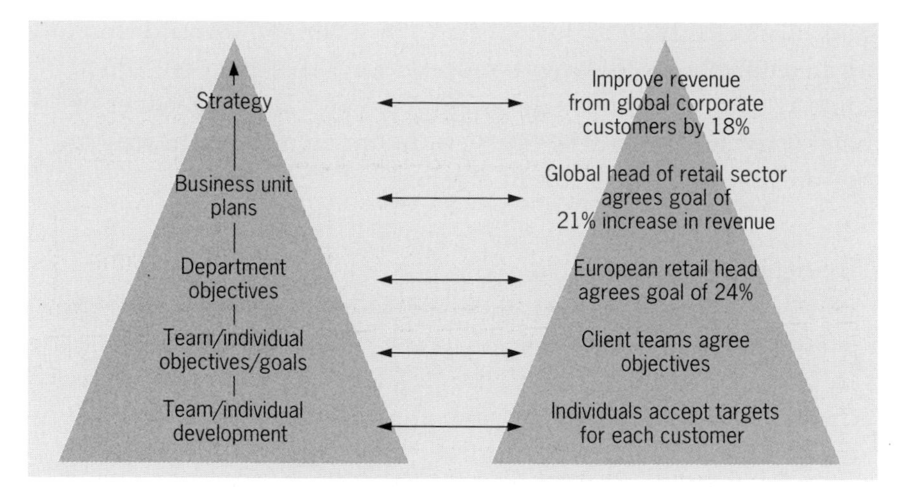

Figure 1.3 *Alignment of effort*

The trend towards expressing organisational values as well as objectives, is one that helps employees, customers and stakeholders alike to translate the vision of an organisation into objectives. The values go beyond the financial targets and all encompassing 'world class' type statements. Organisations are judged far more exactingly, not only on their profits and their expected turnovers, but also on their corporate responsibility, their commitment to employees, their 'green' credentials and their sustainability.

The value of values, as many organisations are finding out, is that they contextualise financial targets within a set of behaviours and expectations. These values need to be met when dealing with customers, fellow employees and other stakeholders.

Team and individual objectives need to describe the end-state that should be achieved within a defined period of time. An objective, such as this one, is not an end-state objective.

> Contributing to the building of consensus solutions for safe and environmentally acceptable means of transport.

Whereas, this is an objective.

> Completion of a comparative assessment of the different potentially acceptable means of transport and their environmental impact by the end of the next quarter.

Your role as a leader and manager is to help to create a logical series of objectives and prioritise them for the team. Having agreed the priorities with at your level you need to examine the interdependencies between the objectives.

This will help to determine whether objectives can or cannot be achieved and whether they do or do not relate to divisional or organisational objectives.

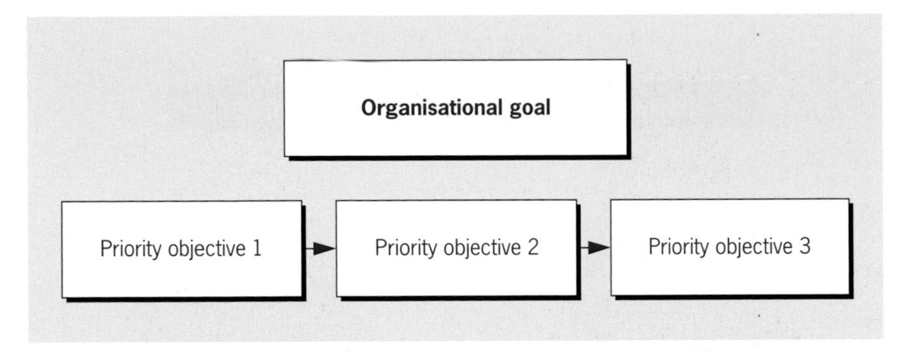

Figure 1.4 *Priority objectives*

It may become evident that some of the objectives are of greater priority than others, or that some objectives are unachievable in their current form. The process associated with drawing up the objectives, when thought through carefully in consultation with the team, should start to highlight how achievable the objectives really are.

Links should also be made to the way the team works and how individual's behaviour fits with the values espoused by the organisation.

So back to the key questions for a manager and their team.

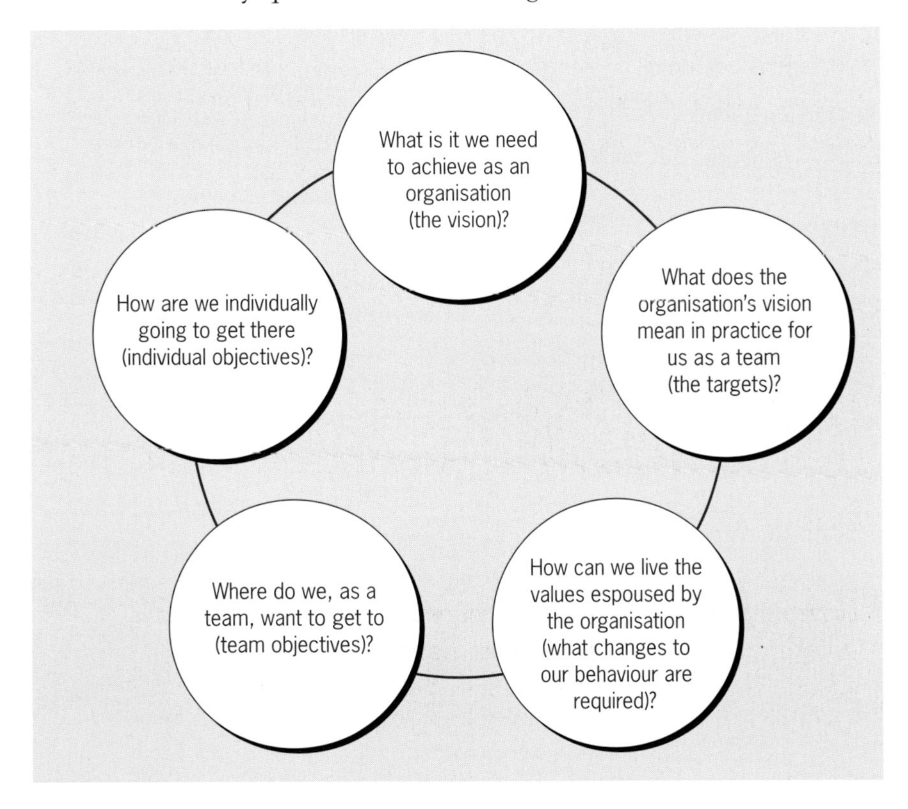

Figure 1.5 *Setting your direction with visions and value*

Developing your objectives in partnership with stakeholders, such as customers, employees or service users is an essential part of getting buy-in and understanding about the future direction for the organisation. Linking them to vision and values emphasises your commitment to the way your organisation works.

Activity 1:
Map your vision and targets

Objectives

This is a visual activity. Your objectives are to:

- map out your organisation's vision
- illustrate what this means to you and your team (and to your team's teams if appropriate).

Task

Your task is to create a visual way of representing your organisational goals, cascaded to your team and individual objectives for your team members.

You can either do this with your team or use the product of your efforts to make a presentation to the team to help them understand the direction they are taking.

If you are confident that your team know their direction ask them to collaborate to help find a useful way to explain this to a new person in the team, a customer or a stakeholder.

Start by envisioning what your organisational mission or vision means to you. What does it mean to you? Why is it important? What messages does it give key stakeholders like employees, customers, users or shareholders?

Add to your picture any strategic and financial priorities for your area of the business.

Now prioritise your own team objectives? What will make a difference in achieving the vision and strategic priorities?

Feedback

Your response will be individual to your organisation, your team and the individuals within it. You should seek to use a visual style that means something to you and the group you are working with. Bounce ideas off each other – it may generate new ideas, and clarify areas of confusion or ambiguity or questions. Keep a note of these and come back to them later. The end result should be clear links between the vision, the strategic priorities for your area and the team objectives.

Setting team and individual objectives

Setting team and individual objectives is more than just agreeing a form of words. Setting objectives involves using skills like negotiation, influencing, coaching, delegation and prioritising. But before you embark on these skills associated with objective setting you'll need objectives that clearly define, both to you and your team members, what needs to be done.

SMART objectives and the Balanced Scorecard

SMART is an acronym which stands for:

Specific

Measurable

Achievable

Results oriented

Time-related

The key is to create an unambiguous statement which is specific and which has a time span associated with it.

SMART objectives look like this.

1. Reduce response time for enquiries from 2 weeks to 7 working days within 2 weeks of project start.
2. Review mailing arrangements (staffing and procedures) to align with the new response time.
3. Send a short letter to existing customers with an apology for delay and an explanation, within 3 working days. Letter to be signed by the head of operations.

Every SMART objective also needs to link clearly to the team objectives and the vision of the organisation.

Another way of structuring your objectives is through the balanced scorecard system. This takes a number of perspectives on the business.

The Balanced Scorecard was developed by Prof. Robert S. Kaplan and Dr David P. Norton, at the Harvard Business School. It was designed to improve performance measurement systems by providing alternatives to performance measurement exclusively through financial targets. The Balanced Scorecard sets out to answer the question, 'What do we need to achieve and how can we get everyone pulling in the same direction?' It focuses on four key areas.

- Customer satisfaction
- Improving internal business processes
- Learning and developing employees and systems
- Financial targets

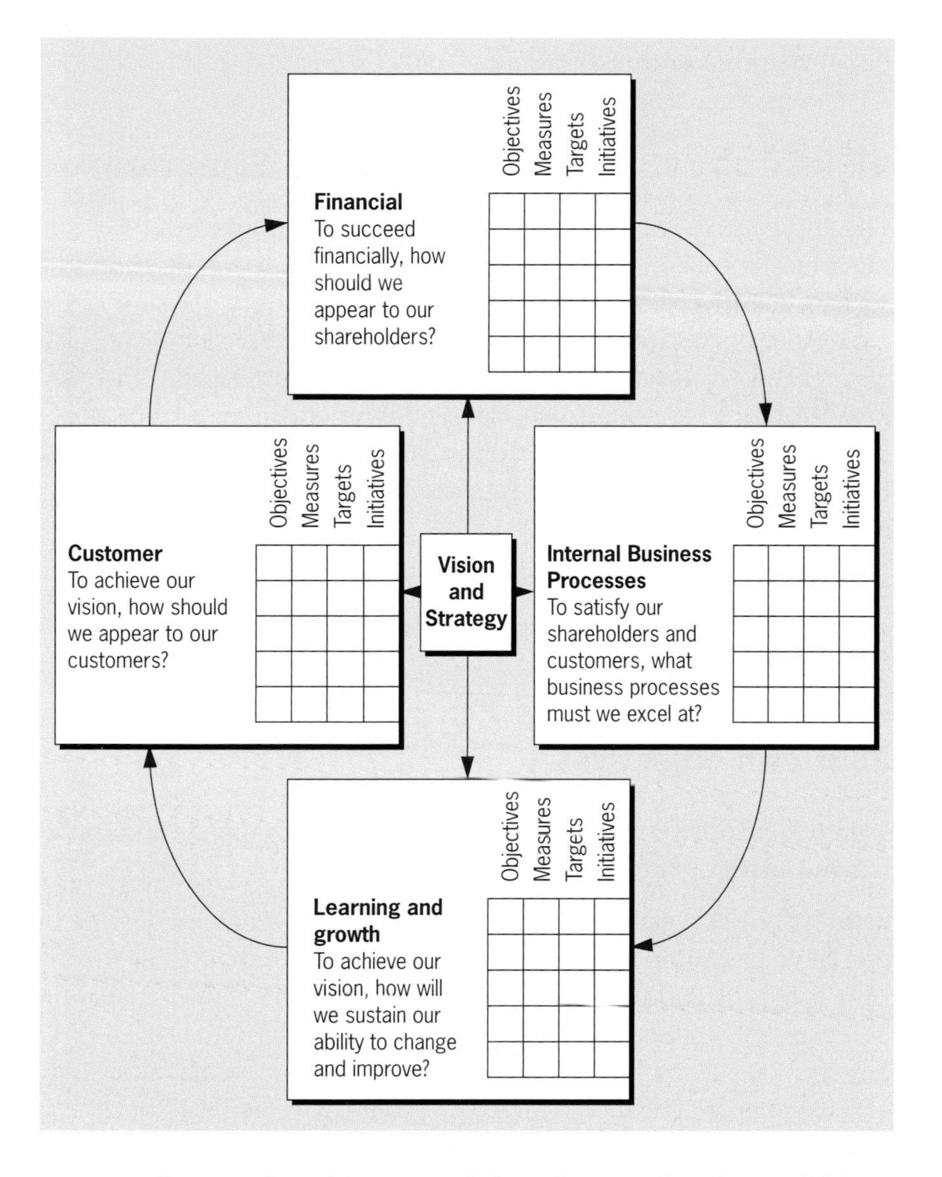

Source: adapted from www.balancedscorecard.org/images/BSC.jpg

Kaplan and Norton describe the balanced scorecard as follows:

> 'The balanced scorecard retains traditional financial measures. But financial measures tell the story of past events, an adequate story for industrial age companies for which investments in long-term capabilities and customer relationships were not critical for success. These financial measures are inadequate, however, for guiding and evaluating the journey that information age companies must make to create future value through investment in customers, suppliers, employees, processes, technology, and innovation.'

The approach uses a feedback loop to measure outputs and outcomes in each of the areas that contribute to an organisation's success. It's an approach that provides information to decision makers, evaluates trends in performance and provides a holistic view of the organisation. It needs to be implemented across the organisation so that managers can see their performance from a range of perspectives. Organisations using this approach will cascade the system down to individuals to make it the basis for setting objectives at every level.

Whatever system is used in your organisation the links between the strategy and vision of the organisation and the objectives of individuals need to be clear.

Your own objectives

Your first priority is likely to be agreeing your own targets and this is where the negotiation starts.

Setting SMART objectives is relatively easy if you are doing it with one of your team members and you are both clear about how much time is required and the skills needed to do the job. As a manager or as a team member your own targets are likely to reflect all the targets of the team. Making them realistic and achievable takes skill and experience. The more you know about the capabilities of the team the more accurate you and the team member can be about what you can expect to achieve.

Whatever your relationship with your manager it is worth formalising the process of objective setting. The space for ambiguity and false expectations can be vast and damaging to relationships. The skills you gain in agreeing your own objectives will also be useful to you when you are working with your team members to agree their objectives.

You may be in a position to set your objectives yourself and simply agree them with your manager. If this is the case, you would be well advised to ask one of your colleagues to challenge you on the meaning and expectations raised by the objectives you have set. It is not unknown for a n individual to set objectives for themselves only to find they are not living up to the expectations of their manager, because of ambiguities in the objectives.

There will normally be a period of negotiation around objective setting and the following guidelines look at the stages in the process.

Guidelines for negotiation

The ultimate aim of any negotiation is to arrive at a position where both parties feel that they have achieved a win (known as win-win). The next best is something that has been described as BATNA – the Best Alternative To a Negotiated Agreement. It's about working out in advance what you'd ideally like to achieve, what you could concede and what are your minimum requirements.

The stages in the negotiation process typically look like this:

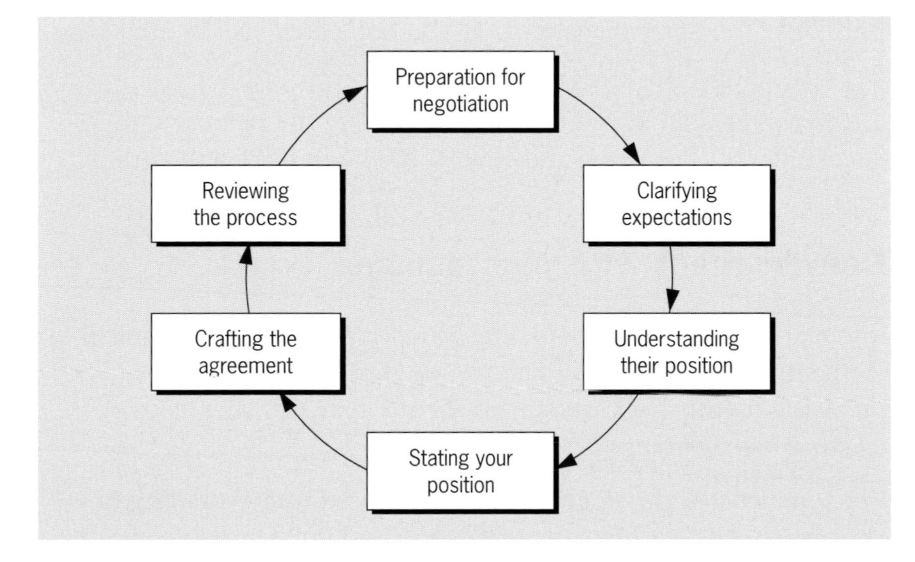

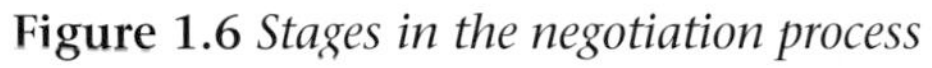
Figure 1.6 *Stages in the negotiation process*

The starting point for any negotiation of objectives is to prepare. Managers need to prepare what they want to achieve, to establish their personal vision in some cases, for the way the team is run. This needs to be set within the context of any concrete targets being set by the organisation. Think about the consequences of not getting what you plan to achieve in terms of the task, the individual and the team.

The second stage is to clarify expectations. The process described above for translating vision into objectives and getting those agreed with other managers lays a good foundation. You also need to look at how team objectives and your own objectives work together to achieve results. Be clear at this stage what resources you will need, especially if additional resources are required. It's worth being specific and having some examples of the kinds of things you want to do, ready to discuss with your manager. At this stage you'll be taking an objective look at the situation finding out what each other thinks.

The third stage of effective negotiation requires you to know and understand what your manager is trying to achieve and to find out what specific behaviours and skills they have used successfully in the organisation. You might also be able to find out the behaviours and values they particularly value. By tuning into your manager, you will be able to understand their perspective.

The fourth stage is about stating your position and listening to the position of your manager. If it gets difficult at this stage, try to resist saying anything – take time out if emotions start to get in the way. Remember what you are trying to achieve the try to understand the position that your manager is taking.

The fifth stage is about crafting your agreement. It may be a simple process or it may have been difficult to reach. The key here is not to make any assumptions. It's easy to think that the negotiation has been achieved and that you both understand your objectives and priorities. This stage demands that you both demonstrate that you really do agree and you recap the objectives in writing.

The sixth stage is simply a matter of reviewing the process and checking what went well and what could be improved next time.

Conversations with your manager

Michael Watkins, in his book *The first 90 days*, outlines a number of 'conversations' that a new manager might have with his boss. They provide a useful checklist of areas for any manager in a new or existing managerial role.

The situational diagnosis conversation – is about understanding how your manager sees the current situation and what you and your boss diagnose as the principle areas requiring attention.

The expectations conversation – is concerned with how you and your manager can best work together and what you are expecting to accomplish in the short and medium term.

The style conversation – is concerned with how you and your manager interact – what style of reporting would suit you both, how hands on will your manager be, what kinds of decision does your manager want to be involved in, how do your styles differ. Even managers that have worked together for a long time may benefit from this approach.

The resources conversation – examines what resources you have and what you will need to achieve the objectives that you are negotiating.

The personal development conversation – is easily missed amidst objective setting. It is concerned with objectives that will help you as a manager to develop. It could be in the form of coaching, training or learning programmes, special assignments or new projects.

The next stage in the objective setting process is to agree objectives with individuals in the team.

Negotiating team and individual objectives

The aim here is to agree clear objectives and targets. Objectives need to reflect:

- current performance
- skills, behaviours and attitudes
- team targets and objectives
- any organisational values.

Managers may also want to add objectives that contain a 'stretch value'. This means they should take effort to achieve, but not be unrealistic. For example, it may be possible to bring a project in ahead of schedule or achieve a x% increased customer satisfaction rate. Objectives should always include a 'by when' element.

Example of 'stretch value'

Current objective:

> Reduce response time for enquiries from 2 weeks to 7 working days within 2 weeks of project start.

Stretch value:

> Reduce response time for enquiries from 2 weeks to 5 working days within 2 weeks of project start. This includes ensuring that the enquiry is logged from first contact with the organisation.

No organisation can afford to stand still. Whether the organisation is in a period of consolidation and stabilisation or in a dynamic state of flux, teams and individuals need to prove to their managers and key stakeholders that they are striving to make improvements to the service or product and the efficiency of their work.

Negotiating with team members

When agreeing and prioritising workloads with members of your team you may be involved in complex negotiations. You need to make sure that work is done to customer requirements; at the same time, you need to ensure that individual members of the team are happy with their workloads, and not working under undue stress;

you have to ensure that work is spread on an equitable basis throughout the team. Your skills in these negotiations are crucial both to the effectiveness and the quality of the working atmosphere of your team.

The process of negotiation with team members is essentially the same as for a manager with their manager. The better prepared you both come to an objective setting meeting the more effectively you will understand each other's position and reach agreement.

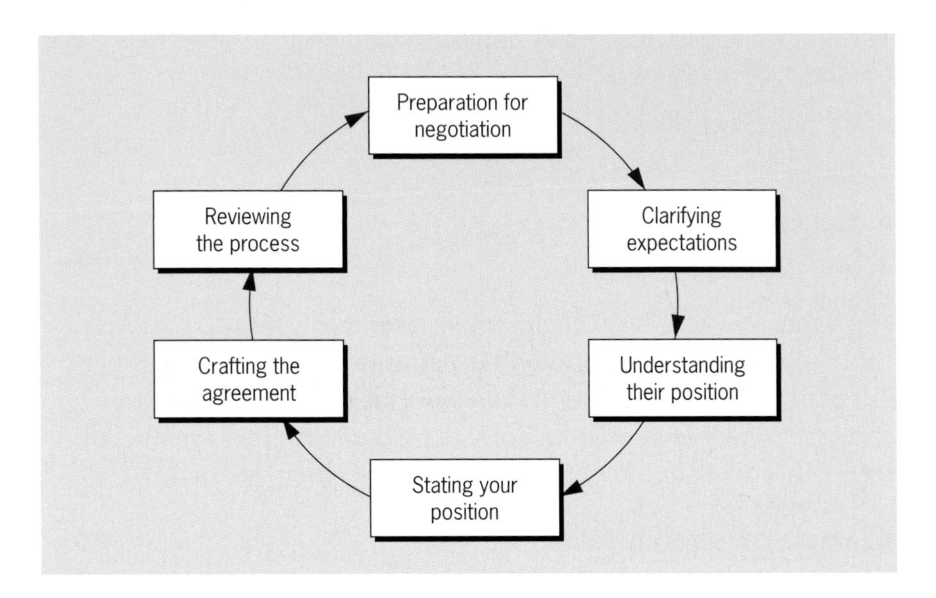

Figure 1.7 *Stages in the negotiation process*

From your position, it is worth taking the time to ensure that team members are well prepared, that they understand what their current objectives mean, how they will be measured and what your expectations are. If possible, ask individuals to set their own objectives, but you'll also need to have a clear idea of what you want them to achieve. Where managers set objectives for their team it is advisable to give them the objectives well in advance so that the individual has time to ask questions and fully appreciate the implications of the objectives.

As a manager it is essential that you are clear about the support an individual is likely to require to fulfill their objectives. An individual may require coaching, training or development to support them in achieving their objectives. The resources need to be in place or at least agreed before they sign up to the objectives.

Involving individuals in the process of their own objective setting will improve understanding of your expectations and the expectations of the organisation. It's a good time to gain commitment to the values, which underpin the vision and direction of the organisation and review the types of behaviours that contribute to those values. With this bigger picture, they will be able to grasp the implications of the objectives they have been set or will be able to set their own SMART objectives.

Maintaining accountability

Responsibility may lie with the individuals within your team for their objectives. Accountability on the other hand still rests with their manager. Accountability means being willing to stand up and be counted. Underlying this is a requirement on you to provide a context of values which help define how the organisation does things in an ethical way. You will need to provide a level of monitoring sufficient to ensure that targets and objectives are being met. By delegating and handing out responsibilities a manager is not abdicating responsibility, instead allowing enough leeway for the individual to carry out their tasks and activities in their way.

Activity 2
Conversations about objectives

Objective

This activity is about structuring your conversations with your manager or your team members.

Task

Look at your existing work targets or objectives, or the targets for one of your team members. Think about Michael Watkins' 'Five Conversations' and imagine you are preparing to have the conversations with either one of your team or your own manager. What are the key points you would like to get across?

The situational diagnosis conversation

The expectations conversation

The style conversation

The resources conversation

The personal development conversation

Feedback

Michael Watkins was using these conversations to set the context for a new manager in their first 90 days in the post. How relevant did you find them? Consider whether you have had conversations with your manager or team members that roughly fit this pattern in the past.

Did planning for these conversations help you to see anything in a new perspective? Would you advise any of your team members to use these kinds of conversations to help develop a productive working relationship with a manager or to help them be clear about what they want to achieve and how they want to do it?

Try out some of the conversations in a meeting you have planned. Then write notes in the space below about what went well, what didn't go so well and what you could improve.

Delegation

'I not only use all the brains I have, but all I can borrow.'

Woodrow Wilson

Woodrow Wilson was clearly making the most of the people around him. But first, let's consider the implications of not delegating.

Signs that your delegation is failing include:

- team Motivation or Morale is low
- you are always working late
- your team is confused, in conflict or tense
- you too often get questions about delegated tasks.

Don't under estimate the importance of delegation. It's not a way of off-loading surplus work; it is first and foremost a motivational tool. It will help others to understand their own capabilities and give you time to focus on strategic priorities.

Delegation allows your team members to use and develop their skills and knowledge to the full potential. Without delegation, you lose their full value.

I delegate myne auctorite'

Palsgrave, 1530

As Palsgrave suggests delegation is about, not only handing over the task, but also passing on the responsibility and the authority. That's not an excuse to abdicate accountability, it's more concerned with entrusting your authority to others.

As a manager your role is to give your team members all the tools and support that will enable them to get the job done without letting anything go badly wrong.

Successful delegation depends on having three foundations in place in the working environment:

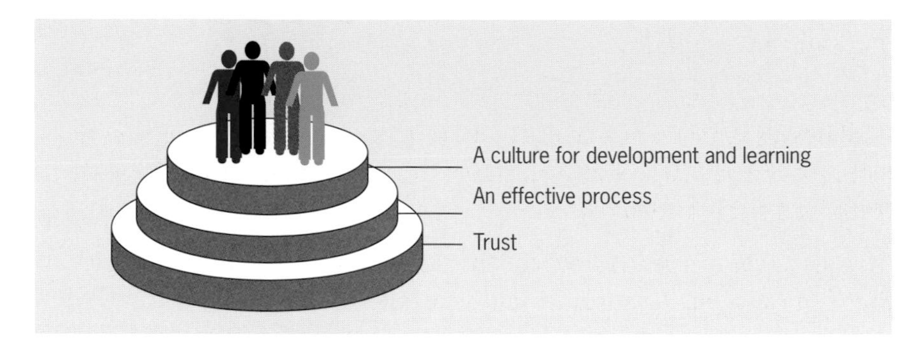

Figure 1.8 *The foundations for successful delegation*

Trust

As the responsible manager you ultimately 'carry the can' for anything that occurs or doesn't happen within your area of responsibility. Managers therefore tend to delegate to people whom they trust, and the degree of control they exercise is directly related to the trust they have in the individual.

The aim is to initiate a spiral of trust within the team – a spiral that encourages openness, listening, respect, creativity and commitment.

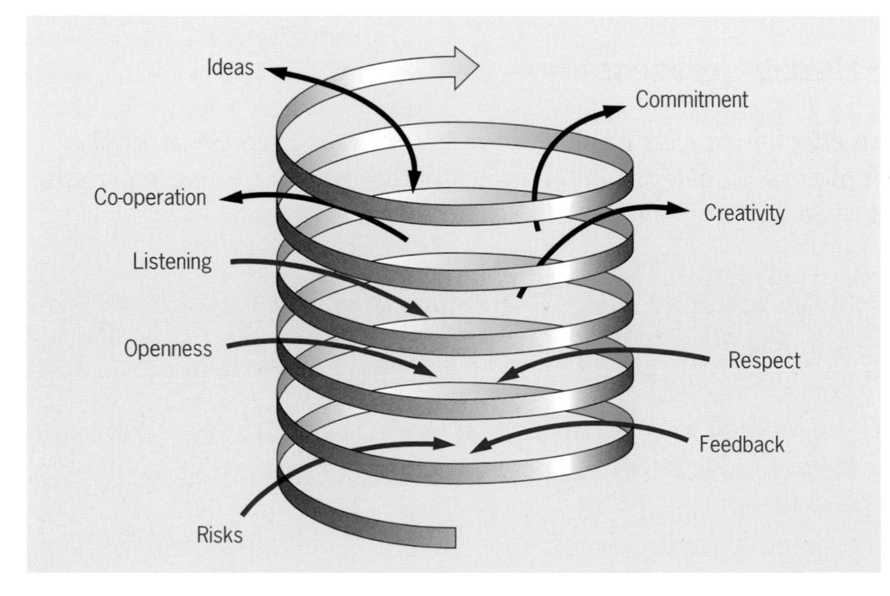

Figure 1.9 *The spiral of trust*

Trust needs to work both ways and some of the ways you can use to gain trust from your team and therefore have trust in them are listed below.

Open up – say what your really mean, be truthful and keep team members informed about everything related to their work, without overloading them with unnecessary information.

Be consistent and objective – treat people equally and be fair by basing and communicating your decisions on the facts rather than on feelings.

Do what you say you'll do – avoid committing yourself to anything you can't or won't do.

Admit failings and mistakes – if you can be open about your weaknesses your team may have an opportunity to help and will feel more inclined to admit to their own, giving an atmosphere of truth and straight dealing.

Give ownership – means letting others make the decisions and give them the support to ensure their decisions work.

Give feedback and credit – your feedback must be honest and constructive. By publicly giving credit you are also assigning credibility over to the member of your team and thereby giving them authority.

Link activities to wider goals – it's no good delegating tasks that don't matter. It's essential your team members understand how the tasks they are delegated link to organisational goals and objectives.

Establishing your trust in the team and their trust in you is not a simple or quick process. It needs to be worked on continually. With trust, a manager is able to let go in the knowledge that work will get done. Without trust a manager is unlikely to hand over the stimulating work and will probably 'micro-manage' the process.

Effective process

An effective process for delegation is essential. There are a number of models for delegation but typically they follow this basic pattern devised by Mullins (1999).

Identify the tasks that can be delegated

Start by considering **what** you can delegate. Factors to consider include the following:

- Avoid delegating tasks that are urgent or have to be completed in a hurry since you will not have time to work through the delegation process.

- The task should be worth doing, so that the person you ask to complete it develops a sense of ownership and pride in carrying out the work.
- You should not delegate any task that carries statutory or legal implications, or which your superiors expect you to do yourself.
- Do not delegate tasks that could create dissent within your department, for example it would be inappropriate to ask one team member to take on a job that involves dealing with the confidential files of other team members.

Allocate the tasks to the right people

The next step is to identify **to whom** you can delegate a task. A large part of successful delegation rests on matching the right person to the right task. Consider whether the person you want to take on the job:

- has a workload that allows them to carry out extra work
- has indicated that they want more responsibility, more challenges or new skills
- has some background experience that is appropriate to the task
- is willing to undertake training if necessary to complete the task.

Brief the person or people involved

When you have selected the task and the person to whom you want to delegate it, you need to prepare a brief that states clearly what should be achieved. The length and comprehensiveness of the brief will depend on the confidence and experience of the person who is taking on the task.

When you explain the task, make it clear:

- why the task is necessary
- what should be achieved
- what the person you have approached will gain from it in terms of experience and satisfaction
- what authority and resources are being delegated
- where they can get help if they need it.

Although the brief should be clear, you do not need to spell out how the job should be done. Delegation involves letting people take ownership of a task and therefore finding their own ways in which to complete it. You should, however, be willing to offer suggestions if they are asked for, discuss ideas and provide feedback.

Support and monitor performance

During the period when the task is carried out, you should offer support, if it is needed, and monitor the task or project to make sure it stays on track. The extent to which you get directly involved will depend on the competence and confidence of team members, how much trust you have in their abilities, how well they are responding to the challenge and how much you can bear to stand back. Ideally, you will keep your distance and only get involved if you are asked to. Constant interference negates the whole delegation process.

Give feedback

Once the task is completed, review it with the person to whom it was delegated. In this way you 'close the loop' by using the experience as a learning exercise. In particular, consider:

- what went smoothly
- any problems that arose
- how the person you delegated to responded to the challenge
- further opportunities for delegation that could arise in the near future.

Development and learning

Delegation isn't just about passing on tasks for others to do. A key element of effective delegation is that the new tasks are stretching and mean that your team members are developing their skills.

It's about creating a culture of development and learning in the team. These skills are the foundations for creativity and innovation, which will support growth in the organisation. The most common reasons not to delegate are about the willingness of managers to invest time in members of the team.

- You may lack confidence in your staff and feel that there is no one to whom you can delegate.
- You believe it's quicker to do the job yourself than to train or monitor others.
- You are afraid of losing control and being superfluous yourself.
- You work in a hierarchical culture where delegation is not encouraged or managers are seen as controllers.

If this is the case, a manager will be missing out on the opportunity to reduce their own workload longer term and increase motivation and self-reliance in the team.

The sort of culture that promotes delegation is also one that sees **all** members of the team:

- supporting and helping each other develop
- looking for learning opportunities
- admitting mistakes.

The questions you need to ask are not only 'What tasks can I delegate?', but also 'What development needs do team members have to meet their individual objectives?' To answer, you have to:

1. know the behaviours, skills and knowledge required to meet the objectives
2. know the competence and confidence of the team member in applying the behaviours, skills and knowledge
3. identify where the gaps (i.e. development needs) are.

In a team with a culture of continuous improvement there are a variety of ways to develop. For example by:

- coaching team members
- team members coaching their colleagues
- you delegating increasingly more responsible tasks
- using self-study materials
- team training sessions
- learning by experience.

The most important aspect of development is to ensure that the skills that have been developed are used and practiced in the workplace.

Delegating projects

Projects are a special case for delegation. They represent an opportunity to hand over a contained and significant piece of work to an individual or team. As such, the preparation required to hand over effectively should be more precise and comprehensive.

Defining the terms of reference for a project involves five main areas for consideration. These are the areas that you need to work out before you hand over. It's worth making them the framework for a discussion with the project team.

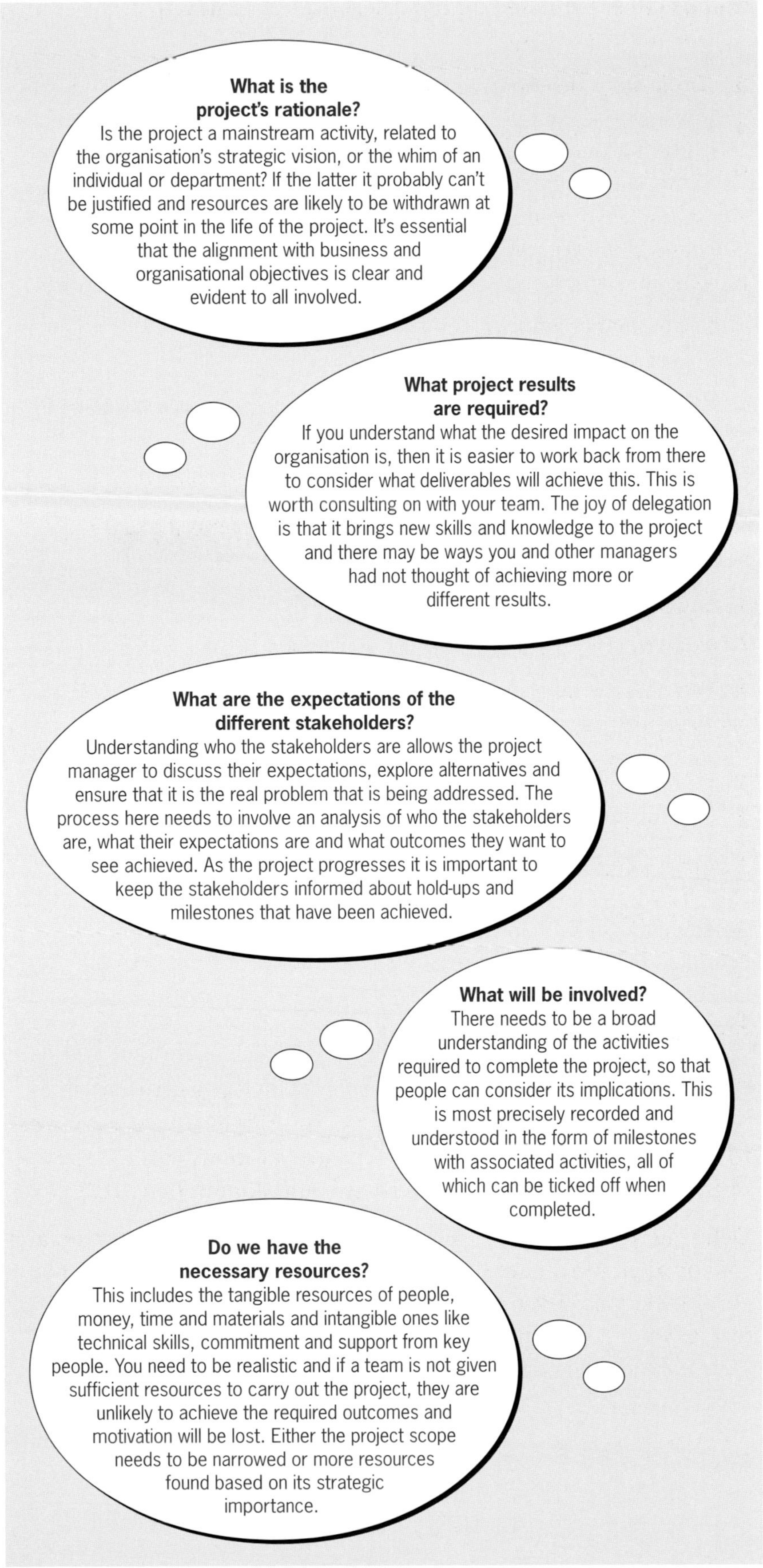

What is the project's rationale?
Is the project a mainstream activity, related to the organisation's strategic vision, or the whim of an individual or department? If the latter it probably can't be justified and resources are likely to be withdrawn at some point in the life of the project. It's essential that the alignment with business and organisational objectives is clear and evident to all involved.

What project results are required?
If you understand what the desired impact on the organisation is, then it is easier to work back from there to consider what deliverables will achieve this. This is worth consulting on with your team. The joy of delegation is that it brings new skills and knowledge to the project and there may be ways you and other managers had not thought of achieving more or different results.

What are the expectations of the different stakeholders?
Understanding who the stakeholders are allows the project manager to discuss their expectations, explore alternatives and ensure that it is the real problem that is being addressed. The process here needs to involve an analysis of who the stakeholders are, what their expectations are and what outcomes they want to see achieved. As the project progresses it is important to keep the stakeholders informed about hold-ups and milestones that have been achieved.

What will be involved?
There needs to be a broad understanding of the activities required to complete the project, so that people can consider its implications. This is most precisely recorded and understood in the form of milestones with associated activities, all of which can be ticked off when completed.

Do we have the necessary resources?
This includes the tangible resources of people, money, time and materials and intangible ones like technical skills, commitment and support from key people. You need to be realistic and if a team is not given sufficient resources to carry out the project, they are unlikely to achieve the required outcomes and motivation will be lost. Either the project scope needs to be narrowed or more resources found based on its strategic importance.

Figure 1.10 *Key questions for project planning*

Mullins (1999) summed up the delegation system well.

> In order for a delegation system to work effectively, staff should know exactly what is expected of them, what has to be achieved, the boundaries within which they have freedom of action and how far they can exercise independent decision-making.

It is a 'system', which only works when planned for and applied effectively.

Activity 3
What could I delegate?

Objective

Use this activity to help you identify some acceptable tasks or projects that could be delegated.

Task

Run an ideas session with your team on the topic of 'What could I delegate?'.

The aim is to get as many ideas and thoughts out as possible, regardless in the first instance of their feasibility. You can assess their feasibility later.

Your task is to find out:

- more about what your team would enjoy doing, what responsibilities they would like to take on

- three potential tasks or projects that could be delegated that link directly to team and organisational objectives

- any barriers to delegation from you or your manager's point of view and from the view of the team.

Feedback

There are a number of good reasons for reviewing the delegation of tasks.

- The tasks may be unusual or different and broaden the team's capability or understanding in a new area.
- You may have made assumptions about an individual's willingness to take on a delegated task or role.
- You may find that people respond to delegation in a different way from that you expected – either positively or negatively – which may lead you to reassess your expectations of an individual.

- Delegation of tasks and roles can be a good testing ground for individuals being considered for promotion.
- Delegation, especially of responsibility and authority can be very motivating and lead to a greater atmosphere of trust.

If you have completed this task with your team you may have opened up new avenues of thought, found new tasks to delegate and uncovered unknown skills and capabilities in your team.

Monitoring the outcomes

Monitoring provides the feedback you need to ensure that projects, tasks and activities are going to plan. But what does monitoring involve and how can you ensure that you are not interfering?

The kind of monitoring you do will depend to a large extent on the type of performance or results you are monitoring. However there are a number of common denominators.

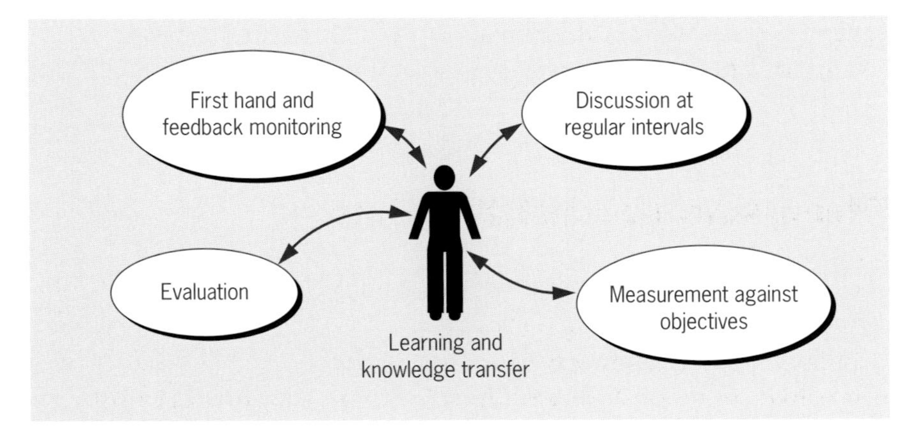

Figure 1.11 *Monitoring work*

Discussion at regular intervals

A discussion pre and post delegation and at regular intervals is essential. This is not about checking-up. It's more about finding out if there are any delays you need to know about and offering support or resources as required. The discussion needs to be open, honest and clear to be effective. Prior to hand-over of a task the discussion needs to clarify objectives, resources, the level of support you can offer and an agreement on when progress will be reviewed. It's worth thinking through some examples of situations when you need to be alerted to a delay or an over run or something that will impact on other members of the team.

The other element of this discussion is to clarify how you will know when objectives and the results expected by a range of stakeholders have been achieved.

First hand and feedback monitoring

Another level of monitoring that may sit alongside the regular discussions or be in addition to them is feedback monitoring. The feedback can be from others in the team, stakeholders, customers or the individuals involved. Whoever provides the feedback, those involved in carrying out the activities need to know that the feedback is being sought, from whom and at what intervals. Informal feedback may be gained on performance by taking the time to talk to people involved – sometimes known as management by walking about.

The feedback could be quantitative or qualitative depending on the nature of the task. You may need to gather both. You might be looking at the way someone is running a project and dealing with the people involved as well as dealing with the hard performance data.

Systems monitoring may be used to gather data on performance or outputs, such as cost, budget and project management systems. Alternatively, formal reports can be used to gain feedback on progress.

Measurement against objectives

All measurements of performance and monitoring should be against well-defined objectives and standards of service. Objectives that are difficult to monitor may need to be redrafted to clarify what is being measured. Self-monitoring is one form of measurement against objectives and is a form of monitoring widely used in areas such as education and the public services. It is based on the premise that those who are involved on a day-to-day basis know best the pitfalls and failings of the processes currently in place. It does, however demand a culture of openness and honesty to be truly effective.

Any review of progress should focus first and foremost on progress against objectives whether they are expressed as SMART objectives, milestones or activities. Contingency plans need to be in place to help sort out any problems as they arise. At the very least an individual needs to know when something that they do will impact on the progress of other projects or activities.

Evaluation

Evaluation of the processes of review should uncover areas for improvement. If things went wrong, in spite of the monitoring taking place, what were the causes and how could monitoring be changed to pick up problems earlier? Evaluation should take into account the views of major stakeholders such as colleagues, managers and customers to ensure a wide perspective is achieved.

Learning and knowledge transfer

This is an area that is sometimes forgotten in the process of monitoring and control, but it is central. Learning and knowledge transfer will contribute to the success of future projects. Individuals need to understand:

- that their new skills and knowledge are valued
- skills and knowledge or new product knowledge should be shared with colleagues
- more responsibilities may be assigned in the future on the basis of their success – this will be a motivator
- monitoring systems may change as a result of the process and individuals involved
- others in the organisation will be informed of the new knowledge and skills gained in the department.

Learning and knowledge transfer are also an integral part of innovation for growth which we discuss in the next theme.

Activity 4
Designing systems for delegation

Objective

Your objective is to set up a monitoring process for your next delegated activity using one or two of a range of monitoring techniques following the framework below.

Task

Use this framework to identify the objectives, support, resources, results and review process for a delegated activity and then choose how you will monitor and review progress.

SMART objectives

How, when and with whom will you devise objectives?

The objectives for the activity are:

What support is required?

What resources are required?

What results do you expect to achieve?

When will you review progress?

From each of the following forms of monitoring choose one or two that are appropriate to the delegated activity and plan how you will monitor it.

First hand and feedback monitoring

☐ Who will provide feedback?

☐ Quantitative feedback – what kinds?

☐ Qualitative feedback – what kinds?

☐ Systems feedback – what kinds?

☐ Formal and informal feedback?

Measurement against objectives

What are your plans for:

☐ Self-monitoring?

☐ Monitoring by the manager?

How will you know when you have achieved the results you expected?

What contingency plans are there to put things right?

Evaluation

Which stakeholders will evaluate the results and the way it was handled?

How will you manage changes to the plans?

Learning and knowledge transfer

How will you support the progress of an individual successful in their delegated activity?

How will you ensure that lessons are learned?

How will you ensure that new knowledge and skills are passed on appropriately?

Feedback

The idea is that you explore a range of evaluation techniques with a view to reviewing the progress and performance of your particular delegated tasks.

As a result of carrying out this activity which of the questions above would you use to help you review progress or outcomes in the future? List the questions below.

Actions

Review the activities you have completed for this theme and write down any action points that you can use to support your efforts to reach your goals effectively.

◆ Recap

Knowing where you want to go is essential and that means mapping out the stages on your journey. This theme looks at the importance of setting objectives that align with your organisational vision and priorities. Negotiating your objectives with your own manager and your team will help you to be clear about your own role in the process.

One of your key tools in reaching your goals is to delegate effectively and then monitor the outcomes. In this way you will be motivating the team and ensuring that you are still heading in the right direction.

Use objectives and targets to help set direction for you and your team

- Clarity of purpose is essential for a well-motivated and self-reliant team.
- When the team objectives contribute directly to strategic priorities the objectives are said to be aligned.
- SMART objectives and the Balanced Scorecard approach are a useful way of getting people pulling in the same direction.

Negotiate objectives to meet organisational needs

Negotiation of objectives involves:

- preparation for negotiation
- clarifying expectations
- understanding their position
- stating your position
- crafting the agreement
- reviewing the process.

You could try using one or more of the five conversations to help you in your negotiations with others.

Understand how delegation will help you and your team achieve objectives

Successful delegation depends on building trust, using an effective process and developing and learning from the experience.

The process is to:

- identify the tasks that can be delegated
- allocate the tasks to the right people
- brief the person or people involved
- support and monitor performance
- give feedback.

Monitor the outcomes

There are a range of monitoring methods including:

- discussion at regular intervals
- first hand and feedback monitoring
- measurement against objectives
- evaluation.

The purpose of monitoring is to learn and transfer knowledge as well as achieve the desired outcomes.

Kaplan, R. S. and Norton, D. P. (1992) 'The balanced scorecard: measures that drive performance', *Harvard Business Review,* Jan–Feb pp71-80

The Balanced Scorecard method of Kaplan and Norton is a strategic approach to performance management, that enables organisations to translate a company's vision and strategy into implementation, working from 4 perspectives:

- Financial perspective.
- Customer perspective.
- Business process perspective.
- Learning and growth perspective.

You might also like to try searching balanced scorecard on the internet or try www.balancedscorecard.org

Watkins, M. (2003) *The first 90 days,* Harvard Business School Press

This book is a road map for taking charge quickly and effectively during critical career transition periods. It's also offers an interesting set of questions and guidelines for managers in post and out of transition periods. You can find out more about the conversations with your manager.

Full references are provided at the end of the book.

2 Organisational Dynamics

Innovation is probably the single biggest factor determining who succeeds and who fails anywhere in the world
Nick Donofrio, IBM Corporation

Although innovation is generally perceived to be positive, it continues to be problematic for many organisations. Why are some innovation efforts successful while others fail? Why does the process that works in one context, meet resistance and rejection in another?

Global competition, new technology and customer demands mean that most organisations need to change, develop or grow. Innovation is an element in that growth and development process. This theme examines the dynamics of organisations and the role of innovation in supporting growth. It also examines the central issue of making innovations work in practice and how to promote and support creativity.

> Innovation is a critical issue for senior executives. A survey of 400 companies found that 70% of companies' mission statements and top objectives mentioned innovation.

Source: Watson Wyatt Survey, 1998

In this theme you will:

- **review the organisational context for innovation**
- **understand how innovation and operations need to work together to improve quality**
- **identify the conditions needed to encourage creativity.**

Why innovation succeeds or fails

> The nature of innovation is changing dramatically in the 21st century. Proprietary invention in search of purpose is out. Open, collaborative and multi-disciplinary approaches to innovation are taking centre stage in the shaping of new ideas and creation of tangible value for business, individuals, and the world.

Source: Global Innovation Outlook, 2005, www.ibm.com

At one time, you might have found an innovation team within the research and development department or a team tasked solely with searching out new ideas. These days such teams may exist, but they are more often part of the mainstream, their skills are permeating through the organisation. Collaboration is the goal.

There is a good reason for this. Ask most people about their organisation's reaction to their last good idea and unless they implemented it themselves, they will look wistfully and say 'in the end of course, nothing happened'.

Barriers to change and innovation

A major programme of research into innovation is being carried out by the Open University Business School. One set of findings relates to barriers to innovation. Unsurprisingly, resource constraints are a major barrier, but beyond this, most of the factors identified were related to people and basic attitudes to change and openness. Examples include:

- people working in their narrow boxes (the silo mentality)
- fear of the consequences of failure (the blame culture)
- lack of perceived adequate rewards for the risk
- hoarding of the best people by unit managers
- people operating in a formal (bureaucratic) way
- 'not-invented-here' attitude (at the implementation stage)
- poor organisational communication
- reluctance to relinquish an erstwhile successful product
- technical obsession/insufficient customer orientation
- a 'business-as-usual' preference and priority over innovation
- short-termism – too strong an emphasis by key players on return on investment.

Most organisations have these barriers to a greater or lesser extent. These are the factors in an organisation that can prevent change and broader thinking.

So, what's the best way to introduce, change, innovation and development into your organisation?

Evolution or big bang

The first Eureka moment

Archimedes had failed to find a way to measure the volume of a gold statue. To relax, he took a bath but filled it full to the brim. As he got in, he realised that the volume of water overflowing would equal his own volume. His 'Eureka moment' linked the previously unconnected ideas of overflowing bath water and a gold statue's volume.

The spotlight is on innovation in many organisations.

Since 'Innovation' became a sexy word for big business, companies have been tripping over themselves to become more innovative. Some merely take a marketing approach and add a slogan that emphasises innovation without bothering to actually become more innovative. Others struggle without succeeding.

Source: Big and little innovation – www.jpb.com/creative/index.php

The question is do you put all your efforts into finding your next star performer or do you look for the little incremental improvements that will make a difference, but may be not make your fortune?

Evolutionary innovation theories can be plotted on a continuum ranging from 'Big bang' or radical to routine and incremental innovation.

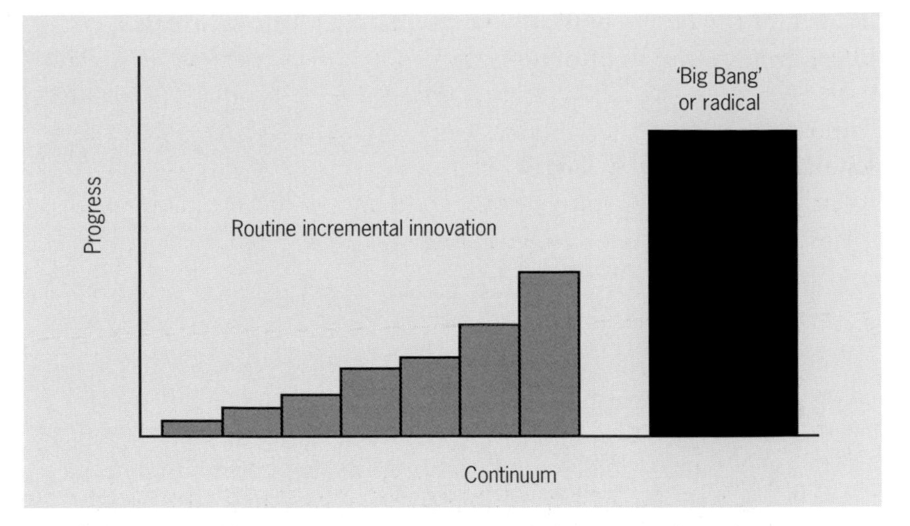

Figure 2.1 *Evolutionary theory continuum*

Ettlie (2006) describes a number of positions along the way. You'll find concepts like punctuated equilibrium where organisations achieve incremental changes punctuated by breakthroughs, which either improve or undermine a product or service. Moving to the left there is the 'jolt theory of change'. This means that organisations change only when they are jolted from their environment, changes that might jeopardise their markets or technologies. Somewhere towards the middle are innovative regimes described by Nelson and Winter (1982). Innovative regimes are normally strong, technological regimes that actively strive to innovate and set-up organisation-wide frameworks for creating and implementing new ideas. Ettlie talks too about architectural innovation described as 'the changes in the subsystems and linking mechanisms that are necessary to obtain the best benefit from minor technological changes. The essence of all these types of change is that organisations are continually learning and gaining knowledge from experience and of technology, markets, customers and competitors, then reformulating the mix of activities they perform.

In *Big and little innovation* Jeffrey Baumgartner describes why incremental innovation is just as important as radical innovation.

> One reason is that most of these companies are looking for a big innovation: that earth shattering new product that will leave the competition in the dust. Such companies overlook small innovations which bring incremental additional income or – more likely – result in relatively small, but nevertheless significant cost savings.
>
> Fortunately, the solution is simple: recognise the value of little ideas.

Source: Big and little innovation – www.jpb.com/creative/index.php

Radical innovation is potentially going to capture or renew a market, but incremental innovation may be more achievable. The size of an organisation will often determine its propensity towards innovation. The larger it grows the more inert and less capable of change it becomes. In large organisations however, there are cultures, people and practices that will support, even generate innovation, and these are generally worth cultivating.

Activity 5

Business dynamics and innovation – what does your organisation look like?

Objective

In this activity your objective is to get a picture of innovation in your organisation.

Task

Answer the following questions about innovation in your organisation.

Is innovation mentioned in your mission or vision statement?

☐ Yes? ☐ No?

How would you describe your organisation's attitude to innovation?

How would you describe your organisation's track record for implementation of innovative ideas?

Does your organisation tend to support big or little innovation?

In what area would you or your organisation most value innovation, i.e. technology, research, marketing, communications, strategy, finance etc?

What are the barriers to innovation in your division or organisation?

Feedback

Much of what you have written about organisational attitudes will depend on the reactions you have had to your own or your team's ideas, the reactions you have seen to the ideas of others or your perception of the organisation.

Show the answers you have written to one or two other people in the organisation, whose ideas may be different to your own.

How do their ideas and attitudes differ?

Innovation is only possible if someone makes it work

The most likely reasons for good, innovative ideas to fail is an unwillingness to put in the necessary effort and the fear of failure. Some organisations see it differently, actively seeking opportunities to integrate innovation into the working environment. The question is what's the best approach. Do you use a random scattergun approach hoping that it might hit a target, or a carefully aimed, slow to reload rifle? The answer may lie in a scattergun with a telescopic sight.

Creating a culture of opportunity

Epstein et al (2005) identify seven rules to support implementation of innovation:

- *Leading innovation* – defining innovation strategy, designing portfolios, and encouraging value creation.
- *Integrating innovation and business strategy* – matching innovation to your overall business strategy.
- *Balancing creativity and value capture* – generating successful new ideas that drive maximum return on investment.
- *Weaving innovation into the fabric of business* – making innovation truly integral to your company's business mentality.
- *Neutralising organisational 'antibodies'* – preventing your company from killing off its best new ideas.
- *Building innovation networks* – leveraging innovation resources both inside and outside the organisation.
- *Measuring and rewarding innovation* – implementing the right metrics and the right incentives to drive results.

Figure 2.2 *Epstein's seven rules to support implementation of innovation*

Source: Epstein, M. et al. (2005) *Making Innovation Work*, Wharton School Publishing

These are typically the characteristics of organisations that innovate on a regular basis. For instance in Silicon Valley they 'build innovation networks'.

> Innovation happens in conversations, not in brains. Silicon Valley, for example, has become a hotbed of innovation because of the way people work and play together, commit to innovate and make successful enterprises together, and organise themselves around thousands of conversational practices, clubs and meeting places.

Source: www.vision.com/offers/how_we_do_it/grasping_opportunity.html

At Amstrad, the technology company created by Sir Alan Sugar, it's about 'leading innovation', hard work and 'weaving innovation into the fabric of the business'. The strength of the company has been in being able to spot the next trend and undercut the price with innovative ideas.

Opportunity is missed by most people because it is dressed in overalls and looks like work.
Thomas Edison

All companies that succeed in an innovative environment are skilled at breaking down barriers to innovation and rewarding success.

There is a process associated with innovation, which can help to move it into the realms of the practical and away from a succession of costly failures.

The process looks like this:

- Understand surroundings and perspective
- Understand the opportunity
- Create a momentum for others
- Make the most of integration opportunities

Each of these are explored in the following sections.

Understand surroundings & perspective

Opportunities can be classified under three general headings, as shown in Figure 2.3.

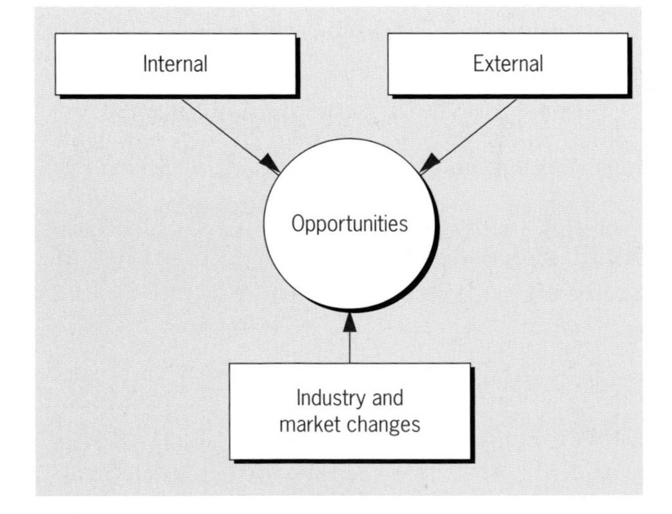

Figure 2.3 *Sources of opportunities*

Internal opportunities

Is it possible to use existing special competencies to create a new business or improve its competitive position? As an example of a company that followed both paths, consider the example of General Electric (GE). The American electrical giant was unable to source suitable materials from the plastics industry so developed its own plastics. Having developed its own special competence, GE marketed the new products, and engineered plastics now form one of GE's major businesses.

External opportunities

The external environment will always offer threats and opportunities. Drucker, considers that opportunities can be found by monitoring seven external sources:

- *The unexpected* – the unexpected success, the unexpected failure, the unexpected outside event
- *The incongruity* – between reality as it actually is and reality as it is assumed to be or as it 'ought to be'
- *Innovation based on process need*
- *Changes in industry or market structure* that catch everyone unawares
- *Demographics* (population changes)
- *Changes in perception, mood or meaning*
- *New knowledge both scientific and non-scientific.*

Figure 2.4 *Drucker's seven sources of innovation*

Examples of innovation in practice

As an example of a process need, consider the benefits for estate agents of the developments of digital cameras and colour printers. They can now produce a colour brochure of a new property within minutes, instead of having to send film off to be processed and then spend time sticking colour photographs onto ready-printed documents.

The development of low-cost airlines depends crucially on changing people's perception of air travel. Early air travel had focused on its luxury aspects but the package holiday industry had enabled many more of us to travel to exotic resorts. Only once sufficient people had come to see air travel as 'normal' was it possible to offer cheap flights without inevitably suggesting that safety and comfort would inevitably be compromised.

Drucker devised that list in 1985. Do any changes since that time suggest new items for the list, or suggest that some areas are now less relevant?

Industry and market changes

According to Drucker, the best sources of opportunities, and the highest probability of success are to be found in opportunities linked to changes in the industry or the market.

The most obvious opportunities linked to changes in industries recently have been in e-business and convergence technologies. Many businesses continue to benefit greatly from taking entrepreneurial-style decisions on adopting e-business, from the video distributor UTube to internet giants like Amazon, from traditional broadcast news to podcasts and blogs.

Increasing legislation in the form of financial reporting, health and safety, diversity and discrimination all have an impact on organisations large and small and demand new ways of working. What can seem like a disaster for some organisations is an opportunity for others. For instance, changes in stock market regulations could have sent shockwaves through the financial world. In fact, they have created numerous opportunities for innovation in stock markets, including regional exchanges with alternative trading venues and expansion into new products not currently traded.

Understand the opportunity for innovation

Marc Andreessen and James Clark developed the internet application Netscape and sold 38 million copies of Netscape Navigator within the first two years: the most successful software introduction ever.

Why did Bill Gates and corporate staff at IBM not spot the opportunity?

> Always remember that someone, somewhere is making a product that will make your product obsolete.

Georges Doriot

It is not easy to generalise about what makes a good opportunity and how to recognise it, but the experiences of successful and unsuccessful innovators suggest a few guidelines. These ideas have been adapted from work by Muzyka in Birley and Muzyka.

- **Value innovation**
  Opportunities are generally about creating value, rather than lowering costs. People will always buy new products if they believe, for example, that they create satisfaction or increase effectiveness. Drucker talks about this as 'delivering value trends'. This is about going one step further than accepting the customer's apparent needs in terms of product. It is about considering the whole package of what the customer buys, including the brand, the services, the guarantees even the system and location of manufacture. It may even come down to an examination of the environmental impact of the product or service.
- **Process innovation**
  Processes can be changed, improved or capitalised on. Complex opportunities for improvement or change often break down. The more stages, and the more people involved, in an opportunity, the less likely it is to be a success in the long run.
- **Product innovation**
  Opportunities are about picking winners from the many ideas that might be suggested for product enhancements or new product developments. They don't need to be radical to be effective. Often the simpler they are the better.
- **Situational innovation**
  Opportunities are specific to the entrepreneur and the situation. Not everyone will pursue an opportunity, or be able to do so. Leonardo da Vinci designed a helicopter in around 1500 but no one successfully pursued the opportunity until Igor Sikorsky in 1939.

Innovation and technology

There is another opportunity that we can add to that list from Muzyka's and that is opportunities arising from new technology. Ettlie lists a number of top technology trends which provide some idea of the impact that technology can still make on the way we all work and the products and services that will become available.

Nanotechnology	This allows manipulation of molecules and atoms and will impact on manufacturing in areas such as silicon chips, transistors, imaging and medical treatments.
Bioinformatics	This is the application of information technology to biological, pharmaceutical and medical problems. It includes areas such as genome sequencing on to chips, making laboratory analysis cleaner, faster and cheaper.
Convergence of digital technologies	Linking telephone, internet, sensors, streaming media and digital images will impact significantly not only on the products and services available, but also on the way we conduct business and our personal lives.
Cryptography	This is about keeping information secure. Already a major issue for organisations it offers enormous potential for innovation and service value, selling via the internet (using digital watermarks for instance), and commercial knowledge management.
Quantum computing	Ettlie proposes quantum computing as the next big thing in computers. The advantage of this kind of computing that is that it acts in a more intelligent way by using probabilities. The effect is that if you change one parameter the computer is capable of recognising a need to change other parameters in accordance. The result is a speeding up of processing power.
Xml	This is the language used in web publishing and the standard for data exchange and now the technology for web services, which makes it the next big trend in application development.
Game technology	This has long been the standard by which other applications are measured. It is being used extensively in training and education.

Table 2.1 *Top technology trends* Source: Adapted from Ettlie, Managing Innovation

Create a momentum for others

The working environment is likely to be a major influence on the motivation for innovation among employees. Tampoe considers that the rewards and expectations of one particular group (the 'knowledge workers' developing new products in the IT industry). They can be summarised as a mixture of:

- personal growth, particularly self-development (rather than growing managerial skills)
- autonomy, having freedom to work within the rules (rather than defining their own rules)
- creative achievement, aiming for intellectually stimulating targets, or commercial targets, that clearly link to the overall aims of the organisation
- financial rewards, particularly salary plus bonus on personal effort (rather than group effort).

On a more general level then what are the features of an environment in which people feel empowered to innovate?

Creative and practical

The balance between creativity and practicality is a difficult one to achieve, but one where a group may perform better than individuals working alone. Some people consider themselves naturally creative. Where this is the case, it is worth encouraging, but not at the expense of all practicality. Some people consider themselves naturally practical – good at getting things done. Both skills are essential to innovation that actually happens. Creating an environment of knowledge and ideas sharing will help the team to create a momentum, which actually goes somewhere.

Playfulness – Developing the good idea

This is the fun element of innovation, which rightly may involve some playfulness to elicit good results. A bit like brainstorming, developing a good idea requires us to breakdown some of the rigidities of our current systems, and thought processes. What's wrong with a few wacky ideas anyway. Good ideas can also be 'imitated' or built up. We are not all pioneers of the next new trend. There are distinct advantages in being an early adopter of other ideas.

Committing resources

Innovation requires resources. To get resources you are likely to have to come to agreement on some parts of the innovative, process, product, system or value added. It may be an organic process of assigning resources as the project builds momentum or it may be that you can argue for resources up front. Either way commitment and momentum are built through the process of providing resources and showing faith in the idea.

Management and reward

Innovation and improvement demand senior level commitment and a culture of reward for effort and achievement. An organisation committed to achieving, growing and improving is more likely to recognise and reward innovative achievements. Employees want their efforts to be valued and recognised openly. The process also demands that managers lead from the front, where possible initiating innovation and improvement processes.

Adjusting to suit the situation

Innovation is generally a response to a new or emerging situation, rather than the discovery or invention of something entirely new. Organisations which actively seek out new trends, technologies and enterprises are more likely to create a favourable environment for innovation. Flexibility in terms of resourcing, people available, attitudes and systems are essential in a group or organisation that wants to capitalise on innovation.

The environment for innovation is a key part of generating a momentum for new ideas, change and growth. Without it people will naturally work towards maintaining the status quo.

Make the most of integration opportunities

Innovation is a learning process, the product of which is new applied knowledge.

> Operations generate today's value, while innovation creates tomorrow's opportunities. The primary difference between operations and innovation is uncertainty. It eludes planning, prediction and containment.

Source: www.1000ventures.com/business_guide/innovation_vs_operations.html

This is a useful summary of the nature of innovation. It is uncertain, and therefore, to many, exciting. To make innovation work in the longer term, what was uncertain, needs the uncertainty removing and regular processes embedded.

Innovation generally works more effectively when it is integrated closely with current working practices. It needs to reflect the vision and strategy of the organisation in terms of focus, differentiation, competitive stance and customer profile. There are some useful ways to ensure that integration takes place.

- Collaborative working is useful to achieve a common aim, thereby exploiting the combined skills and knowledge of all the individuals. Developing team structures that mix skills, that make the most of new ideas and carry them forward, can support this.
- The alternative is to ring fence an area or team with the skills and creativity to generate new ideas. The danger with this is that such a structuring effectively discourages others in the organisation from coming up with process, system or product improvements.
- Integrating an innovation with other ways of working, systems, processes or roles is often a differentiator for success. Innovation needs to be regarded as a process rather than an event or a project. Innovation can be a new way of working in itself; effectively a process improvement. Where the innovation is in a new product or service, the more closely it is aligned to other products or services the more likely it is to capitalise on the skills and processes in place and therefore succeed.
- An evolutionary approach to innovation – which could be in the form of a number of service or process improvements – will often be easier to integrate, to explain and for individuals to make work.
- Discontinuous innovations are often highly disruptive, are more difficult to implement and demand high levels of new marketing commitment and resources.

Activity 6
Innovation SWOT

Objective

Identify how innovation could benefit your organisation, division or team.

Task

Consider the people, resources, culture and information required to exploit innovation? A useful tool to structure your analysis is a SWOT. SWOT stands for Strengths, Weaknesses, Opportunities and Threats. Carrying out a SWOT analysis should help you to make strategic decisions by considering internal strengths and weaknesses and external opportunities and threats. If you know these you can adapt your strategy to meet changing circumstances.

You will need to ask questions like these:

Strengths

- What advantages does your department or organisation have over competitors?
- What do you do better than anyone else?
- What unique or lowest-cost resources do you have access to?
- What do people in your market see as your strengths?

Weaknesses

- What could you improve internally and externally?
- What has gone wrong in the past?
- What are people in your market likely to see as weaknesses?
- Could any of your weaknesses seriously threaten your business?

Opportunities

A useful approach to looking at opportunities is to look at your strengths and ask yourself whether these open up any opportunities.

Useful opportunities can come from such things as:

- changes in technology and markets on both a broad and narrow scale
- changes in government policy related to your field
- changes in social patterns, population profiles, lifestyle changes, etc.
- local events.

Alternatively, look at your weaknesses and ask yourself whether you could open up opportunities by eliminating them.

- Where are the good opportunities facing you?
- What are the interesting trends you are aware of?

Threats

- What obstacles do you face?
- What is your competition doing?
- Are your products or services changing?
- Is changing technology threatening your position?

As a result of your SWOT analysis in which of the following categories can you see the opportunity for innovation:

- Value innovation – opportunities that create value, rather than lowering costs.
- Process innovation – processes that can be changed, improved or capitalised on.
- Product innovation – picking winners from the many ideas that might be suggested for product enhancements or new product developments.
- Situational innovation – innovation specific to the entrepreneur and the situation.
- Innovation and technology – the impact that technology can make on the way we all work and the products and services that will become available.

Feedback

The SWOT is a useful tool in a range of strategic review and decision-making contexts. Come back to your SWOT analysis when you have finished this book and review your answers again. You may also want to show your analysis to colleagues in your organisation. What are their reactions? Has it uncovered any issues that you think may be more important than you had imagined or highlighted any weaknesses that you need to address?

In the space below write some action points that have emerged as a result of your analysis.

Recap

Whatever kind of person you are, if your organisation culture is dominated by a resistance to change – the 'if it ain't broke, don't fix it' type of culture – you're going to have difficulties innovating. This theme looks at your business context and provides strategies for actually making things work.

Review the organisational context for innovation

- Your actions and behaviours, as a leader, are in part driven by the culture and environment of the organisation in which you work.
- A continuum between radical and continuous change is a useful starting point to analyse your past experiences and the current climate for change and innovation in your organisation.

Understand how innovation and operations need to work together to improve quality

- The process for introducing innovation typically looks like this:
  - Understand your surroundings and perspective
  - Understand the opportunity
  - Create a momentum for others
  - Make the most of integration opportunities.

Identify the conditions needed to encourage creativity and innovation

- The key elements of creating a culture of innovation are identified in this theme and examples provided.
- Spotting the opportunity is a crucial first step and Drucker identified seven sources of innovation opportunity, which if monitored, can open up possibilities for change and growth.
- Creativity is promoted in an environment where people are encouraged to grow and develop skills, where they have autonomy, they are stimulated by challenging targets and there are financial rewards. The environment will be one where information is shared and there may be an element of playfulness in the development of new ideas. Ideas also need to be supported with resources and recognition for those who initiate and implement the ideas.

Creativity & Innovation Library
www.jpb.com/creative/index.php

Lots of free articles, papers and tools to help you and your organisation be more creative and innovative.

Drucker, P. F. (1985) *Innovation and Entrepreneurship,* Elsevier Butterworth-Heinemann

Innovation and entrepreneurship deals with 'what, when and why', with policies and decisions, opportunities and risks. The main thesis is that innovation is 'a discipline, with its own fairly simple rules.'

Epstein, M. J., Shelton, R., Davila, R. (2005) *Making Innovation Work: How to Manage It, Measure It, and Profit from It* Wharton School Publishing

Making Innovation Work presents a formal innovation process proven to work at HP, Microsoft and Toyota, to help ordinary managers drive top and bottom line growth from innovation. The authors have drawn on their consulting experience – as well as a review of innovation research. It seeks to demonstrate what works, what doesn't, and how to use management tools to help your innovation work.

Ettlie, J. E. (2006 2nd edition) Managing Innovation, Elsevier Butterworth-Heinemann

Ettlie focuses on a better understanding of the management of technological and organisational change in a global economy.

Full references are provided at the end of the book.

3 Innovation champions and improvement

Not just for heroes

Innovation isn't just about heroes achieving the unattainable against all the odds. It's about you, me and our teams making small steps, working out of the box and following our ideas.

In this theme you will examine on what basis you innovate. Is it because:

1. you have a great idea and a vision to see it implemented?
2. of a natural process of slow stepped changes, which lead to an improvement in quality?
3. learning and past experience inform you about what you need to do?

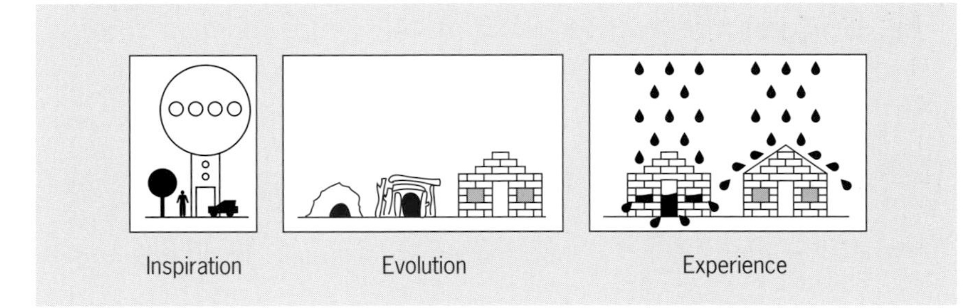

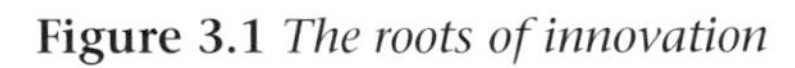

Figure 3.1 *The roots of innovation*

This theme examines what makes an innovator and your role in championing opportunities for innovation. How quality improvement processes can lay the foundation for innovation and a culture that embraces change. And finally it looks at how you can capture learning for continuous improvement.

In this theme you will:

- **identify the characteristics of successful innovators**
- **understand your role in championing opportunities for innovation**
- **review the quality improvements processes that support innovation**
- **understand the processes needed to capture and distribute learning for continuous improvement and change.**

The champions

> A monomaniac with a mission.

Peter Drucker

Peter Drucker's summary of an innovation champion is succinct, but is it necessarily true? Is it possible to work within your current systems, structure and team and achieve innovative change, without monomania?

A salutary tale about a set of people with a form of monomania comes in the form of this story of wasted effort.

> During the heat of the space race in the 1960's, NASA decided it needed a ballpoint pen to write in the zero gravity confines of its space capsules.
>
> After considerable research and development, the Astronaut Pen was developed at a cost of $1 million. The pen worked and also enjoyed some modest success as a novelty item back here on earth.
>
> The Soviet Union , faced with the same problem, used a pencil.

Source unknown – it could be an urban myth

Sometimes the solution is just too obvious and is born out of current working practices.

Here we'll look at the characteristics of successful innovators and entrepreneurs and then at the role of the innovation champion.

The attributes of an innovator

The personal attributes of innovators have been summarised comprehensively by Barbara Mintzer as follows. To consider each of the twelve factors, work through this list to assess your own characteristics:

- Has a compelling vision
- Is opportunity oriented
- Is self-disciplined
- Has a positive, I CAN attitude
- Is passionate
- Is inner-directed
- Is extraordinarily persistent
- Is idea-oriented
- Is a strategist
- Is a trend-spotter
- Takes 100% responsibility for his/her actions
- Surrounds himself/herself with positive people.

Figure 3.2 *Characteristics of innovators*

www.barbaramintzer.com/newsletters/june2004.html

Alternatively:

To innovate is to introduce new ideas and new methods. I believe that an innovator has to demonstrate an ability to look at the accepted, the normal and think 'Why?' 'Why is something the way it is?', 'Why can't it be better?' and 'What can I do to make it better?' – It is this spirit of active questioning that is the essence of Innovation.

Source: Biomedical Research Council, July 2003

The first list of factors was by a leadership consultant, based on a study of her clients and others successful in innovation. The second from the Executive Director of the Biomedical Research Council. You may want to consider to what degree each of these characteristics are essential requirements of an innovator.

Innovation and innovators

Being successful in implementing innovation was also the subject of a study by Peter Drucker (1985). He noticed a number of things about innovation and innovators:

- Innovation is work – it may seem obvious, but it takes a lot of effort.
- Innovators build on their own strengths.
- Innovation is related to the market.

Moving beyond any of these boundaries, he argues, spells failure. For instance to think that innovation is a flash of inspiration that your colleagues will pick up on and run with is wishful thinking in the extreme. However effortless people may make innovation appear, it is more often than not the product of prolonged hard work and preparation. Going back to Pasteur's discovery of germ theory it was the years of patient study that preceded the discovery that allowed him to recognise that a weakened form of a microbe could be used as immunisation against a more virulent form.

Innovators don't innovate successfully in completely unrelated fields using completely unrelated skills. The development of business critical skills and behaviours is central to the role of an innovator. Without analysis, research and determination, innovations just don't get off the ground.

Innovation in a vacuum is also generally a non-starter. There are always exceptions, but in general, innovation that meets or generates a true market need is likely to be more successful.

With these three factors in mind, is it possible for any single person to innovate? The answer has to be yes, but the application of other minds to an innovative approach can reap rewards. By involving a team, considering other ideas and amendments, without losing the power of the original idea, you are more likely to succeed.

What if a member of your team comes up with a great idea, one in which you recognise the potential? How do you develop it further? The concept of the innovation champion follows.

The innovation champion

An innovation champion will be the product of their own personality and style, the culture of the organisation or environment, the team they work with and the innovations they have been involved in.

The personal characteristics of the innovation champion are likely to be varied but typically fairly positive, patient, flexible and determined. The champion will need to be aware how they are perceived by colleagues. For example, they may need to assess the level of credibility attached to them by their team members.

The characteristics of team members will also vary widely. Champions need to know and be able to work with different needs and expectations, attitudes, knowledge, confidence and experience. It's important too to be aware of levels of motivation and commitment.

The nature of the tasks will impact on the style of the champion. Whereas a directive leadership style might be appropriate when managing a task on an assembly line, the leader of an innovative team will often be trying to encourage members to show an original approach. The innovation leader will more often need to act in an affiliative, democratic or coaching style.

The work environment includes both the team itself and the wider social structure and culture of the company. For the leader of an innovative team within a larger organisation, there can be conflicts between differing cultures.

Business Week describes innovation champions as follows:

> They roam the vast spaces of global corporations fighting to make innovation routine, not random; central, not marginal; exciting, not scary. They educate, inspire, cajole, hire, bribe, punish, build — all to transform their companies' cultures.

Business Week picked number of innovation champions and described their key characteristics:

> Every one of them does many things well but one best: Each represents an archetype who builds a culture of creativity in a specific way. There is The Talent Scout, who hires the über-best and screens ideas at warp speed. The Feeder, who stimulates people's minds with a constant supply of new trends and ideas. The Mash-up Artist, who tears down silos, mixes people up, and brings in outside change agents. The Ethnographer, who studies human behaviour across cultures and searches for unspoken desires that can be met with new products. The Venture Capitalist, who generates a diversified portfolio of promising ideas that translate into new products and services.

Source: www.businessweek.com/magazine/content/06_25/b3989421.htm

Thinking about Drucker's innovators, 'building on their own strengths', it is worth considering which kind of innovation champion you might be. Then look at who among you, your fellow managers and your team might fit into each of the roles described.

- The Talent Scout
- The Feeder
- The Mash-up Artist
- The Ethnographer
- The Venture Capitalist.

With an awareness of the style you want to adopt and the roles you require in your team you may find it easier to initiate and carry through your innovation project.

Innovating with a team

Innovating with a team opens the possibilities to bring the best minds and skills to a situation. It could be your opportunity to use your skill-set to greatest advantage, whilst using those of the team to their best effect. It could mean the difference between getting something done and being disappointed at being unsuccessful. Innovation that involves the team is likely to be motivational.

There are four key stages:

- **Stage 1** Understand and develop strategy
- **Stage 2** Develop, evaluate, manage and implement ideas
- **Stage 3** Facilitate group innovation activities
- **Stage 4** Develop and embed innovation processes.

All of the stages need to be inclusive. The team needs to understand and develop their own strategy around innovation or improvement. This needs to be linked clearly to the strategy of the organisation. Team members should be able to articulate how an innovation links to the objectives of the organisation.

A nurturing of ideas is essential so that the team can be sure that their ideas are being acted upon. The key is to nurture and develop as many as possible, but to match the scale of the implementation to the value and feasibility of the idea.

Stage 3 is about facilitating innovation activities as a group. There is a wide range of processes that you can use to ensure a good throughput of ideas. Some of these are explored in the fourth theme in this book. Part of the development of a culture of innovation and improvement is about encouraging learning and the development of ideas to improve or change.

Stage 4 focuses on the processes that you can use to embed innovation in the organisation. This is about checking feasibility and value, risk analysis and decision making processes. The aim is to balance risk against innovation without stifling innovation. This book returns to these processes in particular in Theme 4.

Activity 7
Are you an innovation champion?

Objective

To review a situation and identify some actions you could take to support innovation.

Task

Are you, as Peter Drucker defines a champion, 'a monomaniac with a mission.'? Or someone who champions their own and the ideas of others to make them work?

Consider the following situation:

> Jan has just started working in your organisation after 3 years in Asia. She has a brilliant idea for a service enhancement that is innovative and not currently being used in this country. She has seen something similar working in Taiwan. The service couldn't be used without some adaptation, but Jan is keen that her idea isn't watered down if she takes it to her management meeting. Someone is bound to pick holes in it and it will be undermined. She is researching it keenly, but wants a steer on how to get it implemented. It's all very well coming up with ideas, but unless she can get some action it won't be worth her effort.

You are Jan's manager, how would you support her innovation within the context of your own organisation? Assume that you are able to make a few minor amendments then you are right behind her.

Feedback

The keys to getting something implemented are fairly generic across most organisations. Your response may have included your efforts to support Jan in the following ways:

- Making clear links to organisational strategy. This will be essential if you want to sell it both up and down the organisation. People will need to see how it contributes and will potentially improve something within the organisation.
- Evaluating and developing the ideas with her. This means building on the strengths and eliminating possible weaknesses. It also means assessing where the barriers are likely to come from.
- Facilitating group innovation activities to get the perspective of others on the new way of working. It's about activities like building trust, sharing information, working out potential problems and being creative.
- Working with Jan to develop and embed the process into the organisation. This may mean you have to provide Jan with a high level of support, authority and commitment.

Improvement, collaboration and learning

Things don't stand still. Businesses and organisations are continually striving for growth and better performance. Improvements come in a number of ways, through radical change, stepped change, through the influences of the external environment (dynamic change) and through continual improvement.

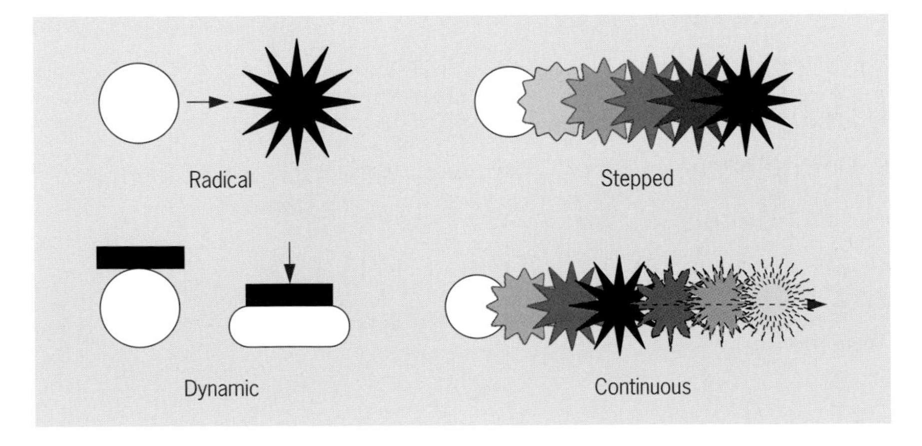

Figure 3.3 *Change in various forms*

What underpins a propensity to change and develop is improvement. With improvement in place, more dynamic and radical change becomes possible opening up more opportunities for successful innovation and growth. In this section we look at the influence of quality improvement, improvement teams and the new influence of collaborative or partnership working.

Quality improvement

Dr Joseph Juran developed a model for quality improvement based on planning, improvement and control. It uses planning to create a structure, techniques like Pareto analysis to improve projects and control to maintain the holds. The model looks like this:

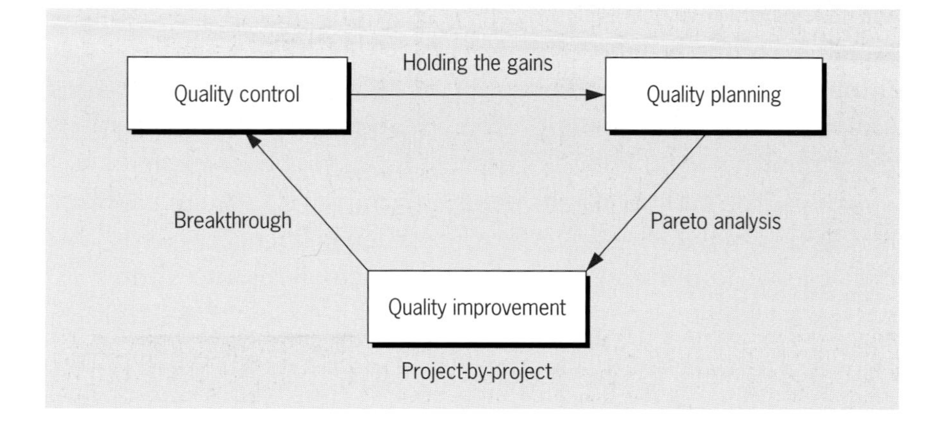

Figure 3.4 *A model for quality improvement*

Source: www.dti.gov.uk/quality/gurus

Juran's model in the Quality Control Handbook (1951) was based on the belief that quality relies on an in depth knowledge of 'customer' (internal and external) satisfaction and dissatisfaction. He saw improvement as a series of small steps.

Quality planning

- Identify who are the customers.
- Determine the needs of those customers.
- Translate those needs into our language.
- Develop a product that can respond to those needs.
- Optimise the product features so as to meet our needs and customer needs.

Quality improvement

- Develop a process which is able to produce the product.
- Optimise the process.

Quality control

- Prove that the process can produce the product under operating conditions with minimal inspection.
- Transfer the process to Operations.

Tom Peters also looked at quality management and identified leadership as being at the heart of quality improvement processes. He talked about 'managing by walking about'. Essentially, he was advocating a process of getting to know people, being available and accountable within the work place. His managers and leaders would ideally be listening, teaching and facilitating.

Quality improvement teams

The adoption of a quality management culture arises from a group awareness of the benefits of improvements in the way work is carried out and the waste that arises. Dr W Edwards Deming focused on Japanese principles of improvement and waste reduction by using the power and knowledge of the teams involved in the processes. The best people, he argued, to improve a system are those involved in making it work. The role of management was to facilitate the improvements, providing structure, resources and encouragement.

Deming's work has been adopted and adapted over the years.

A benchmark set of standards commonly used today is ISO 9000, which sets out the key areas teams, looking to improve, need to review.

Customer focus	Identifying and working towards the specific needs and expectations of all customers.
Leadership	Setting measurable objectives and showing sustainable commitment to quality standards and policies.
Involving people	Ensuring that people at all levels are involved in the processes of improvement.
Process approach	Essentially processes that transform inputs into outputs that are valued by customers – these are usually divided into core processes and supporting processes.
Systems approach	These examine the interrelationships of the processes and the importance of these in making the processes work smoothly.
Continual improvement	Customer satisfaction is in a constantly moving state depending on new technology, the markets and global influences. It is essential to listen to the voice of the customer.
Factual decision-making	Quality depends on making decisions based in reality and on fact through measurement and monitoring of processes and product or service data.
Mutually beneficial supplier relationships	From partnership agreements to straight supplier arrangements the importance of mutual benefits is increasingly seen as a key factor in quality management.

Table 3.1 *ISO 9000 improvement standards* Source: Adapted from www.dti.gov.uk/quality/qms

These are widely recognised as a good point of departure for the planning and implementation of improvements within an organisation.

Collaborative working

Perhaps the greatest shift in recent years has been from team working to collaborative working.

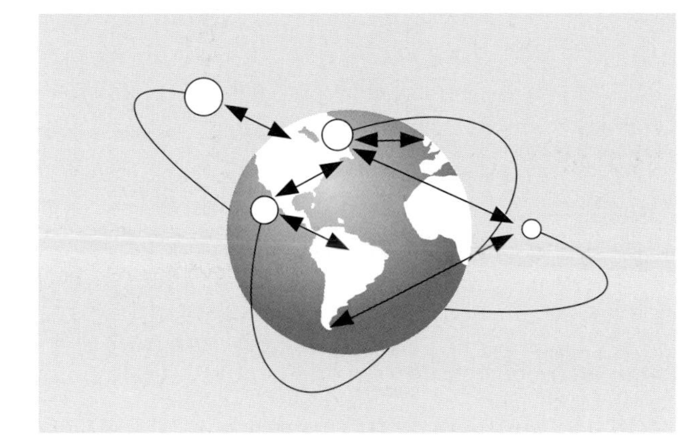

Figure 3.5 *Collaborative working*

Often now used in software development and the arts, collaborative working recognises that although it is important to strive towards 'best practice' it is also unlikely that we can always agree what that is and a range of good practices are a valuable point upon which to build. Many software projects have been notoriously difficult to scope and plan from the outset.

Recently, iterative systems of development such as AGILE (see definition below) have been used. They recognise the difficulties associated with large-scale and complex projects and build in more opportunities for change, improvement and for building on past applications and established practice.

> Most agile methods attempt to minimise risk by developing software in short timeboxes, called iterations, which typically last one to four weeks. Each iteration is like a miniature software project of its own, and includes all of the tasks necessary to release the mini-increment of new functionality: planning, requirements analysis, design, coding, testing, and documentation.

Source: http://en.wikipedia.org/wiki/Agile_software_development

The advance we see increasingly is the recognition that collaboration can occur beyond the skills' boundaries of a single organisation. Improved supplier relationships, partnership approaches and alliances have been the focus of many organisations in the past decade. The principles of mutually beneficial supplier relationships have been, in the case of enterprises like the online encyclopedia Wikipedia, taken to extremes involving a global community of suppliers working concurrently on new iterations.

What are the characteristics then of collaborative workers? They have been variously described, but common characteristics appear to be patience, flexibility, modesty and the ability to multitask whilst working with short-term objectives.

The Ministry Of Defence (MOD) describes collaborative working as follows:

> In simple terms, collaborative working involves using information systems to enable individuals or groups of individuals to work concurrently on information, no matter whether they are dispersed or co-located.

Source:
www.contracts.mod.uk/dc/public/ebusiness/collaborative_working.htm

In this case it is the ability to multi-track, to get people working concurrently that they particularly value to achieve the complex systems required for the design and development of fighter craft. Imagine what this means in the commercial world. Could you envisage EasyJet working harmoniously with Virgin or banks truly working together to fight fraud. Sounds unlikely, but then ten years ago we could never have imagined the popular appeal of an online encyclopedia created by members of the public.

Sharing data and information is a vital component of a true collaborative relationship, enabling:

- those collaborating to add value to data and information by sharing their insights and ideas, discussing options, and raising questions
- members of the team to share activities and actions, and track progress
- people to organise and search for information more effectively and efficiently.

The MOD also cite the following as aspects of an effective collaborative working environment:

- integrated processes
- sharing of tacit knowledge and personal insights
- generation of new and better ideas
- joint problem-solving
- joint risk identification
- faster learning.

Innovation, change and quality are at the heart of improvement, learning and collaborative working. Organisations are increasingly recognising the importance of keeping up with technology, adapting and testing new ideas.

Capturing learning

Capturing learning is essentially about learning from experience and the environment around you. Using mistakes, problems and successes as the catalyst for learning or using environmental scanning processes to monitor trends.

There are two useful theories that have stood the test of time in relation to experiential learning – the learning cycle and double loop learning. This is the kind of learning that helps you to deal with Drucker's 'unexpected' or 'incongruous' situations.

The concept of single and double loop learning was first proposed by Argyris and Schon (1978). The difference being that single loop learning involves the detection and correction of error within the context of their normal operations. Double loop learning on the other hand further questions and scrutinises the limits of normal operations opening the learning up and exploring organisational learning.

Kolb and Fry (1975) put forward their theory of learning as a cycle. They argue that the learning cycle can begin at any one of the four points – and that it should really be approached as a continuous spiral. Strictly, there should be no starting point, but the stages are commonly numbered as follows.

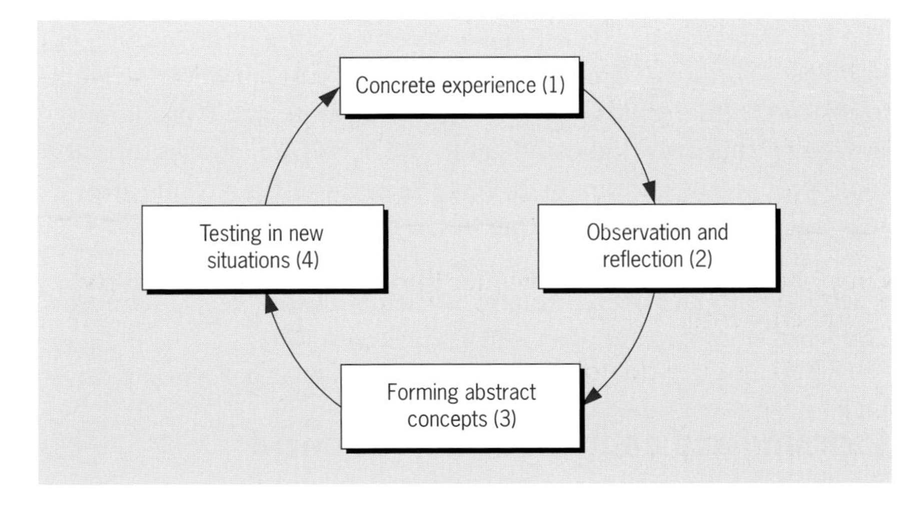

Figure 3.6 *The learning cycle*

Two further ways of looking at learning relevant to organisational growth are Signal and 3R learning.

Signal learning is about gaining information for strategic planning through environmental scanning. The essence is to monitor the environment and interpret the signals being given. Lowe and Marriot (2006 p 124) describe this as follows.

> The organisation gains knowledge about the environment in which it operates and can adjust its strategies accordingly to maintain its position.

As it moves on the organisation may need to incorporate learning in anticipation of, or in response to, critical events from a market – changes in the industry, market or demographic as Drucker would categorise them. Doole and Lowe (2005) established a model of reflect, re-evaluate and respond (3R learning) as a process for dealing with new situations.

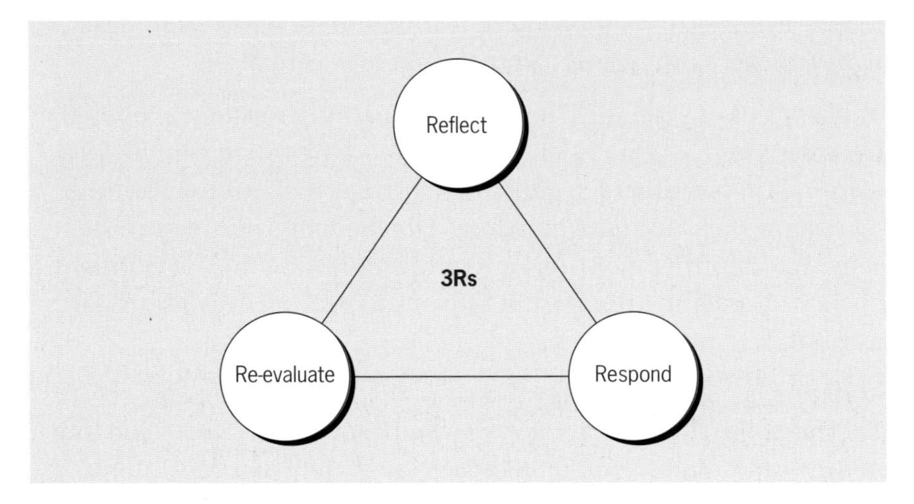

Figure 3.7 *3R learning*

The model challenges traditional ways of thinking in favour of building a culture of learning. This is achieved by questioning what exists and thinking about how it will meet future markets and learning to discard what could get in the way. This releases capacity to do other things. Individuals thus released can then create and seek out new knowledge. In this way, a company develops its internal competence for learning and by doing so is more likely to reach new product breakthroughs, anticipate latent customer needs and learn from its failures as well as successes.

Learning and continuous improvement

Learning contributes to continuous improvement. For instance 'That went wrong last time how can we prevent it happening in the future?' or 'I don't know how to make this work. What is the best way of finding out?' The continuous improvement cycle is a feedback, loop system.

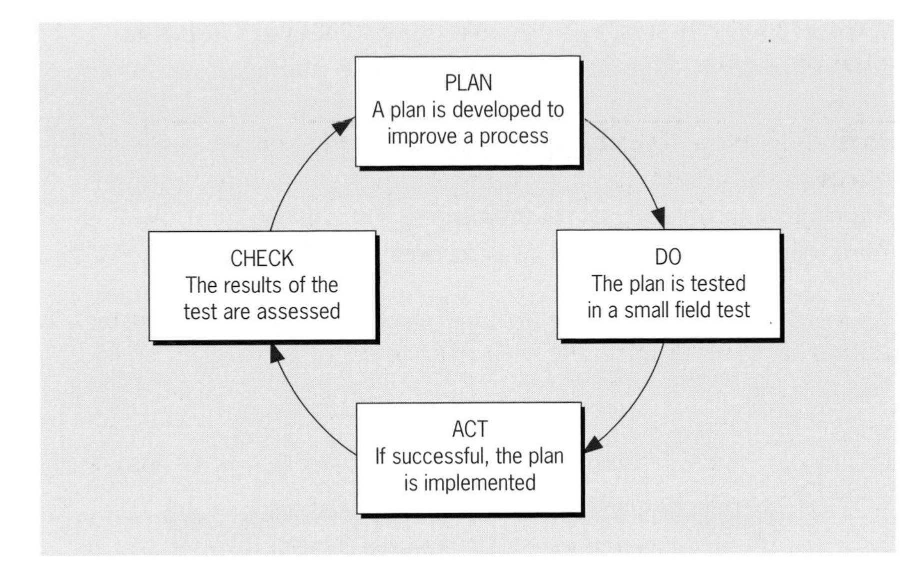

Figure 3.8 *The continuous improvement cycle*

At its most simple it is a never-ending cycle of review. The important thing about continuous improvement is that it is a daily activity something that is continually reviewed.

There are tools that can be used to support continuous improvement activities that focus on post event analysis and learning.

- *Focus group evaluation* – how did a group of users find the project process or the outcome, product or service?
- *Implementation log* – a record of the process and any ongoing difficulties – these can sometimes be forgotten in the excitement of a successful conclusion.
- *Interviews with users* – these can be an invaluable tool for uncovering different ways of approaching a project post event. People are more likely to talk about methods and approaches in a face-to-face situation.
- *Questionnaires* – these can help to gather comparative information to support future improvement.
- *Post project reviews* – are a formal means of measuring outcomes and processes against planned objectives and milestones. They can be formalised into a report or reviewed in a meeting. Either way it is essential that this be seen as a positive process. This can be achieved by using the learning to help envision a subsequent project or piece of work.
- *Critical incident analysis* – critical incidents are those that have an impact on the outcome of the project or activity. The analysis of critical incidents is basically a good starting point for discussion of methods and techniques and improvements that can be made to the process.

Captured learning and continuous improvement are important sources of knowledge and data that will help managers, teams and organisations, not only review current practices, but also find solutions to the problems they don't know they have yet. Keeping ahead of the competition, and perhaps more importantly these days, keeping up with the technology is an essential part of managing the development of your organisation.

Activity 8
Constructing Wikipedia

Objective

This activity will help you to review the concept and practice of collaborative working.

Task

More an act of faith than a clear-cut plan. It's collaborative and it works. Is the Wikipedia model the way forward?

Read the following article from *Time* magazine and consider how collaborative working could have an impact on the way you work with your team in your organisation.

'Edit this page.' Just three little words, but what a miracle they have wrought. Just about every entry on Wikipedia.org, the online encyclopedia, invites visitors to fiddle. Is the entry incomplete? Add something. Is it wrong? Correct it. Is it biased? Edit away. That such a remarkably open-door policy has resulted in the biggest (and perhaps best) encyclopedia in the world is a testament to the vision of one man, Jimmy Wales.

Wales, 39, is a former options trader who in 1999 set out to reinvent the encyclopedia for the Internet age—free, up-to-date and available to all. He started the way most encyclopedists start, by commissioning articles from experts and subjecting them to peer review. After 18 months, he had a pitiful 12 entries; at that rate, it would take a few millenniums to equal Encyclopaedia Britannica. So Wales created a free-form companion site based on a little-known software program called a wiki (the Hawaiian term means quick) that makes it easy—with the 'edit this page' button—to enter and track changes to Web pages. The effect was explosive. That simple button turned readers into contributors and contributors into evangelists. Wikipedia now has more than a million articles in English, nearly 10 times as many as in Britannica. That number nearly doubles each year. And most extraordinarily, the site has not been defaced by vandals or hijacked by zealots. Or more precisely, it is vandalised every day but is usually repaired within minutes by any one of the millions of users who are motivated to protect and nurture the site.

Source: www.time.com/time/magazine/article/0,9171,1187286,00.html
Posted Sunday, Apr. 30, 2006

How could you use the power of collaborative working in your environment?

What barriers might you face?

Who might be involved in the collaboration?

What benefits and improvements could you achieve?

What shifts in culture would you need to make working more collaborative?

Feedback

Collaborative working is whatever you make it and it often succeeds or fails on the strength of personality of a few key managers in the organisation. What works in your organisation may not be the same in another organisation. It's a concept that is being adopted in a range of arenas, from partnership arrangements in the public and voluntary sector, to allegiances and sometimes mergers in the commercial. This is how the NHS Institute for Innovation and Improvement described their approach to collaboration.

> *Effective partnership promotes the sharing of information and appropriate prioritisation of limited resources. It also supports 'joined up' provision of integrated care. The quality of dialogue in collaborative working is critical so that problems can be identified and common solutions agreed.*
>
> Source: www.executive.modern.nhs.uk/framework/deliveringtheservice/collaborative.aspx

◆ Recap

There are a number of different angles you can take on innovation and improvement. Three are explored here. The first angle is that innovation is more likely in a culture that supports change and quality improvement. The second is that innovation comes from the heads of either great minds or champions who recognise great ideas. Or finally, that innovation is the result of learning processes and reviewing one's actions. Which do you and your organisation tend to favour? Or is it a combination of all three?

Identify the characteristics of successful innovators

- Match your own and your team's personal traits to the list of suggested characteristics.
- If that isn't enough there are Business Week's Talent Scout, Feeder, Mash-up Artist, Ethnographer, Venture Capitalist. Where do you stand?

Understand your role in championing opportunities for innovation

- Innovation that involves the team is normally motivational.
- There are four stages in creating an environment for team innovation – understand and develop strategy – develop, evaluate, manage and implement ideas – facilitate group innovation activities – develop and embed innovation processes.

Review the quality improvement processes that will support innovation

- Quality improvement is required on a continual basis because organisations don't stand still.
- Quality improvement works best when teams co-operate.
- ISO 9000 sets out the key areas teams looking to improve need to review.
- Collaborative working is an iterative process and works best when it is not confined to a narrow group of people.

Understand the processes needed to capture and distribute learning for continuous improvement and change

- Capturing learning is essentially about learning from experience and the environment around you. Using mistakes, problems and successes as the catalyst for learning or using environmental scanning processes to monitor trends.
- Captured learning and continuous improvement are important sources of knowledge and data that will help managers, teams and organisations not only review current practices, but also find solutions to the problems they don't know they have yet.

More @

Drucker, P. F. (1985) *Innovation and Entrepreneurship,* Elsevier Butterworth-Heinemann

Innovation and entrepreneurship deals with 'what, when and why', with policies and decisions, opportunities and risks. The main thesis is that innovation is 'a discipline, with its own fairly simple rules.' Chapter 11 *The principles of innovation* is likely to be very useful in this context.

All of the following websites have some interesting and practical information on the implementation of innovation and improvement projects.

www.managing-innovation.com

QFD Institute **www.qfdi.org**

MOD **www.contracts.mod.uk/dc/public/ebusiness/collaborative_working.htm**

DTI Quality models **www.dti.gov.uk/quality/qms**

Full references are provided at the end of the book.

4 Tapping into innovation

Innovation is not an option. It's a necessity. When technology, the environment and attitudes change as fast as they do now, there is less and less room to sit back and reap the benefits of long established 'cash cows'.

Being creative isn't an easy option. As we have seen, we first need to open our minds to the idea that change is necessary through analysis of the current situation. Once this is apparent, we need to start tapping into new ideas and ways of doing things. Katharine Hepburn understood how hard this could be:

> It would be a terrific innovation if you could get your mind to stretch a little further than the next wisecrack.

Source: Katharine Hepburn

Having established your new ideas the next stage is to test them to see if they are feasible, capable of being done with the resources you have, viable, which means of sustainable benefit to the organisation and, if they are, what risks are associated with them?

In this theme you will:

- **use a variety of ways to generate creative solutions and make decisions**
- **use criteria to assess the feasibility and viability of new ideas**
- **understand and evaluate the risks and benefits**
- **build in contingency plans.**

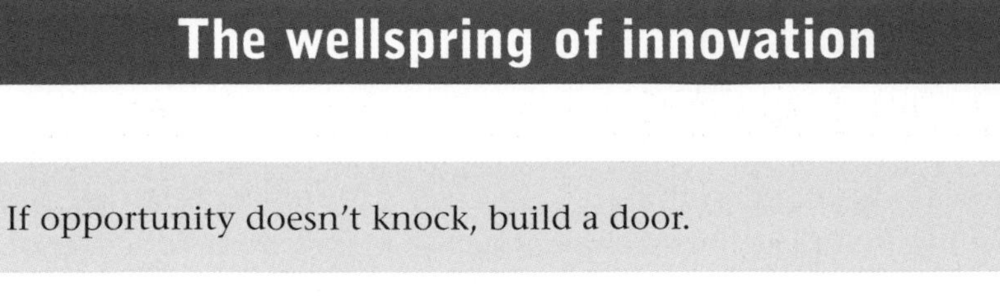

The wellspring of innovation

> If opportunity doesn't knock, build a door.

Milton Berle

Milton Berle's analogy is insightful. Opportunity isn't likely to come to you. You need to find a way to encourage it. The key to this is to be aware of the opportunities available to you.

Innovation and the creative process

The creative process around innovation rests on five planks of awareness.

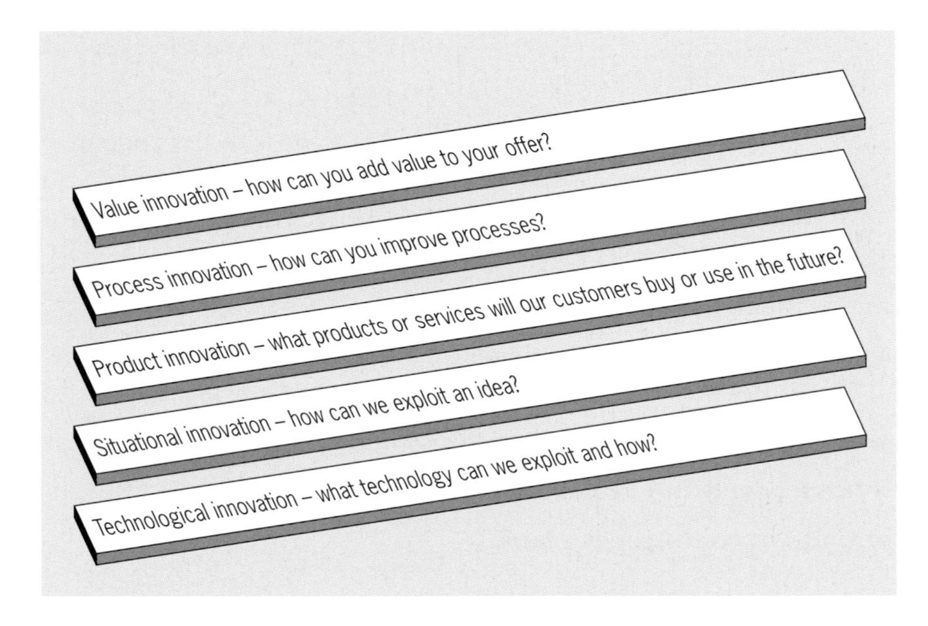

Figure 4.1 *Innovation and the creative process*

Being aware of your environment and the competitive environment is fundamental to the creative process. The following are a set of ideas to help you review the current situation and predict the next. They comprise forecasting, analysis, creative and ideas generating models and tools used in business today. This is a round-up of some of the most effective and you can find out more about any of them by entering the terms into your search engine.

Tools and techniques

	Brief description of some of these tools and when to use them
Brainstorming	This is about generating many and radical ideas in a group. There should be few boundaries to the types of ideas put forward and opportunities need to be created to ensure that ideas are built on, understood and encouraged.
Analogies	Creating links with stories to innovation strategies. In general terms, an analogy is a means of understanding novel situations and problems in terms of familiar ones. Mumford and Porter *(1999, 71-72)* consider analogies as a mapping of similarities between two problems – one problem which is understood is used to help interpret another problem by reorganising ideas and knowledge using the structure of the first problem.
Ansoff Matrix	The Ansoff Growth Matrix is a tool that helps businesses decide their product and market growth strategy. Ansoff's product/market growth matrix suggests that a business' ability to grow depends on whether it markets new or existing products in new or existing markets. ◆ Market penetration ◆ Market development ◆ Product development ◆ Diversification
Balanced Scorecard	The concept of the balanced scorecard is simple. It was invented in the 1990's by Dr Robert Kaplan and Dr David Norton at a time when organisations tended to rely only on financial indicators as a measure of the health of an organisation. They argued that organisations should plan, monitor and measure performance on a more balanced set of indicators – hence the term 'balanced scorecard'.
Benchmarking	Benchmarking is the general name given to a range of techniques, which involve comparisons between two examples of the same process so as to provide opportunities for learning. Benchmarking can, for example, be used to compare how different companies manage the product development processes; where one is faster than the other. There are learning opportunities in trying to understand how they achieve this.
Boston Matrix	This matrix offers a simple technique for assessing your firm's position relative to others in terms of its product range. It is a 2x2 matrix, plotting market share against market growth. The BCG matrix should help you think about the portfolio of products and services that you offer and make decisions about which you should keep, which you should let go of and which you should invest further in.
Business Excellence Model	The Business Excellence Model is a nine-box model, originally developed by the European Foundation for Quality Management (EFQM). The idea is that you improve your results by looking at how you achieve them. The first stage is to conduct a self-assessment, comparing your organisation to the model. The model is based on two key factors – enablers and results. Results are expected in the following areas – financial, customer satisfaction, people satisfaction and impact on society. They are achieved through enablers – leadership, policy and strategy, people management, resources and process management.

Business Process Re-engineering (BPR)	It is about the improvement of productivity by looking at entire processes, rather than at specific activities or functions. BPR is however, often used as a means of getting organisations out of difficulties. More benefits can be achieved if companies are willing to examine how strategy and re-engineering complement each other. That is by learning to quantify strategy (in terms of cost, milestones, timetables); by promoting ownership of the strategy throughout the organisation; by reviewing the organisations current capabilities and processes realistically; and by linking strategy to the budgeting process.
Competence Mapping	Competence mapping is about mapping the knowledge base of the organisation. ◆ It can be used to identify the key areas of knowledge that contribute to the organisation's competitive success, and to help it understand how it might develop or combine these in the future. ◆ It can be used to identify additional competences that would be necessary to move in a new strategic direction. ◆ It is a useful tool in identifying gaps between what the organisation needs to achieve its goals, and the current skills and knowledge set.
Discontinuous Innovation Audit	Joe Tidd, John Bessant, Keith Pavitt (2005) have created an auditing tool which focuses attention on some of the important areas of discontinuous innovation management. Discontinuous innovation is disruptive and may be avoided because of its effects. The results of discontinuous innovation, such as DVDs and microwaves, require a very high investment in marketing to make the customer understand their value.
Five Forces Analysis	The most influential analytical model for assessing the nature of competition in an industry is Michael Porter's Five Forces Model. Porter explains that there are five forces that determine industry attractiveness and long-run industry profitability. These five 'competitive forces' are: ◆ The threat of entry of new competitors (new entrants) ◆ The threat of substitutes ◆ The bargaining power of buyers ◆ The bargaining power of suppliers ◆ The degree of rivalry between existing competitors.
Idea and solution finding	Brainstorming, where a large number of ideas are generated and grouped. Provocations, where the ideas are subjected to comments that are aimed at generating new insights and perceptions. Random stimulus, where physical objects are used to create associations of ideas.
Lateral thinking	Lateral thinking is a term probably originated by Edward de Bono. He defines lateral thinking as methods of thinking concerned with changing concepts and the way we look at things. Lateral thinking is about generating ideas that may not be immediately obvious, taking them out of the normal context or ways of thinking. Stories are commonly used to stimulate lateral thinking, as are provocative questions and word associations.
Pareto Analysis	You may have heard of the 80/20 rule – for instance 80% of the service difficulties are as a result of 20% of the services provided. Pareto analysis can help you prioritise and focus resources where they are most needed. It can also help you measure the impact of an improvement by comparing before and after data.

PESTLE Analysis	PESTLE is a tool used to examine the environment external to your organisation. It can be used for instance in the context of marketing, strategy, new product development, quality improvements and change. P stands for the political context, E for the economic, S for social changes, T for technological changes, L for the legislative environment and E for environmental changes. Using each of these categories as prompts an organisation can evaluate the likely external changes and the impact they will have on the operation and growth.
Product Life Cycle Analysis	The Product Life Cycle method identifies the distinct stages affecting sales of a product, from the product's inception until its retirement. Knowing how the product is likely to perform and using past performance as an indicator of time scales it should be possible to predict when sales are likely to grow, mature and then decline – giving forewarning the of the need to improve, change or innovate the product or service mix.
Product/Process Matrix	The product/process matrix is a simple tool for mapping whether or not proposed choices around your firm's product or service portfolio are in line with your overall delivery capability. Step 1 involves plotting two axes, one for the product or service families that your organisation currently delivers and one for the processes that it uses. What do you make and what processes do you use? This defines the area within which your organisation is operating and therefore the competencies that you are using. Step 2 involves asking whether the new proposal fits somewhere within this space or lies outside it, in other words, somewhere that will require the acquisition of new competency. Products or services outside current competency are likely to be high risk.
Quality Function Deployment	QFD is a comprehensive quality design method that analyses customer requirements. It: 1. seeks out spoken and unspoken customer needs from fuzzy Voice of the Customer verbatim 2. uncovers 'positive' quality that wows the customer 3. translates these into designs characteristics and deliverable actions 4. and delivers a quality product or service by focusing the various business functions toward achieving a common goal–customer satisfaction. Source: QFD Institute www.qfdi.org
Stage Gate Models	Radical innovation involves a huge amount of risk. Most organisations and individuals prefer to mitigate that risk by implementing a series of stages by which to measure responses and test feasibility. There is a range of stage models, but many include concept definition, market research, planning integration into existing processes and systems, testing stakeholder satisfaction and monitoring. The idea is to change the gamble into a set of managed risks.
Strategic Positioning	Given that the external environment changes rapidly strategic positioning is concerned with mapping the impact therefore an organisations response to the changing conditions. It uses other models and tools in the analysis of the position but principally aims to find out: ◆ what does the future look like? ◆ how could the organisation be positioned in the future? ◆ how are things in the organisation at present? ◆ how can opportunities be seized and how can threats be met? ◆ how can this be put into practice in a systematic way?

Supply Chain Management	Is there anything about the way the organisation manages the supply chain that could be improved and that will lead to better or new products/services. According to the (CSCMP), a professional association that developed a definition in 2004, Supply Chain Management 'encompasses the planning and management of all activities involved in sourcing and procurement, conversion, and all logistics management activities. Importantly, it also includes coordination and collaboration with channel partners, which can be suppliers, intermediaries, third-party service providers, and customers. In essence, Supply Chain Management integrates supply and demand management within and across companies.' The emphasis in supply chain management tends these days to be on developing opportunities for co-operation and collaboration.
SWOT Analysis	SWOT analysis is a framework for analysing your company's strengths and weaknesses, and the opportunities and threats you face. This will help you to focus on your strengths, minimise weaknesses, and take the greatest possible advantage of opportunities available. See activity 6 for more details.
Value Chain	The idea of the value chain is based on the process view of organisations, the idea of seeing a manufacturing (or service) organisation as a system, made up of subsystems each with inputs, transformation processes and outputs. Analysis of how value chain activities are carried out determines costs and affects profits. The analysis can highlight weaknesses and strengths, as well as opportunities for improvement. Porter divides an organisation into primary and secondary activities. According to Porter (1985), the primary activities are: 1. Inbound Logistics – relationships with suppliers and all the activities required to receive, store, and use inputs. 2. Operations – all the activities required to transform inputs into outputs (products and services). 3. Outbound Logistics – all the activities required to collect, store, and distribute the output. 4. Marketing and Sales – activities which inform buyers about products and services. 5. Service – includes all the activities required to keep the product or service working effectively for the buyer after it is sold and delivered. Secondary activities are: 1. Procurement 2. Human Resource management 3. Technological Development 4. Infrastructure.

Table 4.1 *Creative and analytical tools and techniques*

Source: List of tools adapted from www.managing-innovation.com

Your role is to use these tools to help you develop, evaluate and implement new products, services or processes to improve and grow your business.

Objective

This activity will help you to get a strategic perspective on the external environment factors that are likely to impact on you and your organisation in the future.

Task

You have looked at your organisation or department's strengths, weaknesses, opportunities and threats. You are now going to have a look more widely at the external environment with a PESTLE.

P stands for the political context, E for the economic, S for social changes, T for technological changes, L for the legislative environment and E for environmental changes.

Using each of these categories as prompts evaluate the likely external changes and the impact they will have on the operation and growth of the organisation.

Political context

Economic context

Social context

Technological context

Legislative context

Environmental context

1. Which of the environmental factors are affecting the organisation?

2. Which of these are the most important at the present time? In the next few years?

Feedback

This is a very broad ranging analysis, but one which will give you a good overview of where you are going. The factors are prompts to get you thinking. Did you manage to uncover any new issues in your analysis?

It is important that the implications of the factors are understood. You may have identified a number of drivers of change likely to affect your industry, sector or market. You will need to examine some factors separately and then look at the combined effect of these separate factors. Other factors you will need to deconstruct to identify the implications. For instance, look at the range of forces which are leading to increased globalisation of industries and markets. The impact on all organisations is potentially enormous and needs to be looked at more closely to break down individual factors.

It is particularly important that a PESTLE analysis is used to look at the future impact of external factors, which may be different from their past impact and their current impact. Using scenarios may help with this. Scenarios are used to identify a number of possible alternative futures and how you might get there. They show how different interpretations of the driving forces of change can lead to different possible futures.

PESTLE analysis may also help to examine the differential impact of external influences on organisations either historically or in terms of likely future impact. This approach builds on the identification of key trends and asks to what extent they will affect different organisations.

Feasibility and viability

Feasibility and viability are about evaluating ideas – how technically feasible or possible are they to achieve and how sustainable are they for the organisation? How can you quickly determine whether an idea is likely to work?

Feasibility

The answer is basically that ideas that work need to be grounded in an analysis of the idea, the market, new knowledge and the attractiveness of the ideas to the organisation or business leaders. You need to explore whether you can make your ideas work. Here we look at analysing the market, focusing the idea, starting small and resource analysis.

Analysing the market

The analysis needs to be based on a number of questions relating to the organisation, the individuals involved, the team, the industry and the market. These have been summarised as follows:

Is the opportunity consistent with the company's strategy?

Note that this refers to the long term strategy; it is quite likely that a new opportunity will not fit with current capabilities and that new resources (financial, plant or staff) will be needed. Note also that some opportunities may be so desirable that a 'spin-off' venture is worthwhile, for example in the same way that Yamaha Motors developed from Yamaha Musical Instruments.

Will the factors that produced the opportunity last?

Think about the turbulence of share prices, the rapid development of new technology and changes in customer spending behaviours. All of these can have an impact on opportunities.

What are the market characteristics?

Here the key factors can be summarised as:

- the size of the market niche or segment in relation to the size of the company
- the life-cycle stage of that market and current rates of market growth
- the size of the likely market share
- the degree to which the product can be protected, for example through patenting or unique technologies
- the expertise of the company in that market; this is particularly important if the company is considering moving into a new business, for example when Sainsbury's moved into internet banking.

Is the opportunity worth the effort?

Some guidelines for innovators can be gained from the venture capital industry. They will typically look for the following economic characteristics:

- a break-even time of less than 36 months (though this period will vary depending on the type of market and the product)
- stable gross margins of 20 to 50 percent
- after-tax profit potential of 10 to 15 percent
- investments are made in stages rather than in one shot
- low asset intensity (this will not be possible in certain markets, for example bio-technology or semiconductors)
- differentiation on product rather than price.

Is the operation feasible?

A key question is whether the company has knowledge and experience in the proposed industry or market. If not, possible approaches would be to gain that expertise through employing new people, acquiring a company that does have that expertise, or taking a small, preparatory step into the market to gain experience.

Timmons has summarised the key areas that you'll need to think about in evaluating an innovation as follows:

Industry and market	*Economics*	*Competitive Advantage*	*Harvest issues*
Customers	Time to break-even	Fixed and variable costs	Value added potential
User benefits	Return on Investment	Controls over costs and prices	Exit mechanism
Value added	Capital	Barriers to entry	
Product life	Internal rate of return		*Management team*
Market structure	Cash flow	*Strategic differentiation*	Entrepreneurial team
Market size	Sales growth	Degree of fit	Relevant experience
Growth rate	Asset intensity	Timing	Integrity
Market capacity	R&D expenditures	Technology	Intellectual honesty
Market share attainable	Gross margins	Flexibility	
Cost structure	After tax profits	Opportunity orientation	*Personal criteria*
		Pricing	Goals and fit
		Distribution channels	Opportunity costs
		Room for error	Risk/reward tolerance
			Stress tolerance

Table 4.2 *Evaluating innovation*

Not all the factors will be relevant and some may be more relevant than others. You can use this table to identify the factors that make the venture particularly attractive and those that make it less attractive. Identifying a fatal flaw will, of course, be a deflating experience, but at least you will be able to stop the venture, or make changes, before expending more time and resources.

Focusing the idea – go out, look and ask

Your perception of an idea is key to its forward movement. It can also be its biggest barrier. You are likely to be in one of two situations, reviewing an idea that is proposed to you or proposing an idea that you or you and your team have developed.

Either way your attention should be directed towards honing the idea and asking for the opinion of others. Some feel nervous about the asking for opinions, fearing that their ideas might be stolen or the credit given elsewhere. It happens, but rarely, and more importantly if you want to make your idea work you're going to need the commitment of others. If they have a say in the direction it takes they are more likely to buy in. Drucker (1985) proposes the following process based on a study of successful innovators.

> Successful innovators use both the right and left sides of their brains. They look at figures, and they look at people. They work out analytically what the innovation has to be to satisfy an opportunity. And then they go out and look at the customers, the users, to see what their expectation, their values, their needs are.

Starting small

Again, from Drucker's principles of innovation, successful innovators, he proposes, try to do one specific thing. Smaller innovations take less money, fewer resources and are capable of more targeted marketing. Giant leaps typically take higher and longer investment and people may lose the plot in the process. If you can describe your innovation clearly and without complication, you're more likely to convince leaders of the need to invest.

Resource analysis

Resource analysis is a tool that looks at what you've got around you to help you implement your new idea and whether it will help you integrate and focus or unduly divert your attention. The sorts of questions you may need to ask look like this:

Physical resources	◆ What plant or equipment do we have or will we need? ◆ How does possession of this plant give us competitive advantage?
Human resources	◆ What skills do we have, and how many people have them? ◆ How adaptable and innovative is our workforce?
Financial resources	◆ What are our relationships with our shareholders, banks and other providers of finance? ◆ Financial strength can be a source of competitive advantage allowing a company to pursue strategies not open to its competitors.
Intangibles	◆ What goodwill does the company possess? ◆ This may be the firm's greatest asset, particularly in a service organisation.

Table 4.3 *Resource analysis*

Source: Adapted from Johnson and Scholes (1999)

A basic check of the fit between what you do and what you are proposing is useful in convincing others that their lives and businesses will not be turned on their heads with the introduction of your new idea.

Viability – The key decision

Is it viable? In other words is it sustainable? This is the question you are going to need to be able to answer to convince your team to get involved, to raise funds, and gain investment or commitment from leaders or financiers. The analysis you have undertaken in assessing feasibility will inform your presentation of your idea's viability.

Viability depends on a number of factors that will vary according to your organisational context.

Viability factors include:

- cash flow forecasting – how will the innovation fit into the existing and revised forecasts for cash flow?
- the type and volatility of industry you are in – in the computer industry for instance volatility and rapid adoption of new technology are common
- experience of previous innovation – whether your organisation is risk favourable or risk averse
- return on investment (ROI) – for the capital and resource outlay what will be the return in terms of profit and turnover?
- net present value calculations – a standard method for evaluating competing long-term projects in capital budgeting. It measures the excess or shortfall of cash flows, in present value (PV) terms, once financing charges are met. All projects with a positive NPV may be undertaken
- payback period – which measures the time required for the cash inflows to equal the original outlay. It measures risk, not return.

An analysis of relevant factors will be required in the development of any business case to support an innovation. The aim is to evaluate the idea for associated costs, returns, initial investment and the period in which payback can be achieved. Where these are positive the implementation of an innovative idea is likely to be successful.

Being Devil's Advocate can also be a useful way of approaching viability. It might prepare you for the 'dragon's den' of getting funding, time or resources to implement your idea. To prepare for this a useful tool is a force field analysis.

Force field analysis is a way of examining all the forces for and against a decision. You are effectively weighing up the pros and cons.

Example of a force field analysis

Weight for	*Forces for*	*Forces against*	*Weight against*
5 ←	Customers want new product – market research results	May impact on existing product sales	→ 3
2 ←	New technology means we could produce the new product much faster than existing lines	Introduction of new technology is costly	→ 4
3 ←	The new product has more potential for adding customer value services	The resourcing of the new services needs to be reviewed	→ 3
3 ←	Increased brand value associated with the new product	Changes to established market channels may impact on existing lines	→ 2
	Introduction of a new high technology product line		
4 ←	Perception from market research that the organisation would appear to be luddite without the new product	Introduction of a new product likely to disgruntle a small but loyal element of the customer base	→ 2
Total for 17			Total against 14

Figure 4.2 *Example force field analysis*

By carrying out the analysis you can plan to strengthen the forces supporting a decision, and reduce the impact of opposition to it.

How objectively can you assess your idea?

A force field analysis is only as good as the forces you put into it. There are a number of personal pressures that you may feel and should be aware of as a result of your innovative idea. These include:

- the need to satisfy the key stakeholders and, within that group, the shareholders
- corporate pressures to pursue a strategic direction, but at the same time produce positive cash flows from the current business
- cultural pressures from within the organisation to safeguard jobs and the investment that has been made to build-up intellectual capital
- safeguarding, while at the same time updating, the resource base of the organisation
- maintaining relationships with suppliers, customers and distributors
- balancing personal objectives with the interests of internal and external groups
- a concern to maintain a personal image within the organisation and with external groups.

All of these pressures need to be factored in to your assessment of viability.

Activity 10

Looking outside from in

Objective

Feasibility and viability are relatively easy to test if you use the objective measures in the techniques and questions like the ones raised in this section. But how easy do you find it to be objective about one of your own ideas or an idea you are committed to? Here you will analyse your objectivity.

Task

Reflect on your past experiences in introducing new ideas using the following susceptibility chart. This will help raise your own awareness of areas you are vulnerable to the pitfalls of owning an idea.

Pitfalls	*Your susceptibility* 1 Low	2	3	4	5 High
Not matching a solution to the strategic priorities of the organisation	☐	☐	☐	☐	☐
Believing people can do more than they have the skills or time to achieve	☐	☐	☐	☐	☐
Poor understanding of the market	☐	☐	☐	☐	☐
Arriving at a solution before you have identified the problem	☐	☐	☐	☐	☐
Being overly focused on the financial or economic benefits	☐	☐	☐	☐	☐
Being isolated from other departments in the organisation	☐	☐	☐	☐	☐
Sticking to your ideas firmly without letting others suggest amendments or become involved	☐	☐	☐	☐	☐
Ignoring the potential for alliances with others in the organisation	☐	☐	☐	☐	☐
Minimal sharing of information with others in the organisation so that your idea strikes like a bolt from the blue	☐	☐	☐	☐	☐
Letting your ideas become diffused without having a clear idea what you want to achieve	☐	☐	☐	☐	☐
Being too ambitious from the outset	☐	☐	☐	☐	☐
Setting false expectations among stakeholders	☐	☐	☐	☐	☐
Allegiances to particular suppliers or team members that override your judgement	☐	☐	☐	☐	☐
Having a concern to maintain your image or status with others internally or externally – you have a reputation to live up to	☐	☐	☐	☐	☐

Table 4.4 *Susceptibility chart*

You can ask colleagues to rate you as well, but be prepared for some differences of opinion.

Feedback

Some of these pitfalls may seem to contradict themselves like 'Sticking to your ideas firmly' and 'Letting your ideas become diffused'. The aim is to be able to avoid the extremes of any of these situations. It's important to be focused, but not at the expense of being flexible enough to recognise when someone else's contribution might be of value.

Avoiding pitfalls like these will earn you respect and trust from your colleagues and your team. They will be keen to work with someone who is able to critically appraise their own ideas and still have the sense of purpose to get it up and running.

The lower you scored on each of these pitfalls the better. But be honest, because you'll need to be able to criticise your own ideas too.

Risks and benefits

Hell, there are no rules here — we're trying to accomplish something.

Thomas Edison

Are you a maverick risk taker or carefully risk averse? Most of us are somewhere in between. In trying to address risk and benefits Drucker developed some principles to guide potential risk takers.

- Don't try to be too clever – it has to be handled by ordinary human beings.
- Don't splinter – integrate and focus – innovations that stray from the core are likely to diffuse.
- Innovate for the present not the future.

How far do you believe these are relevant to your style of innovation? Is it the simpler the better and the more focused the better? Why can't you innovate for the future?

To answer the last question this is what Drucker has to say.

> An innovation may have a long-term impact; it may not reach its full maturity until twenty years later. The computer, as we have seen, did not really begin to have a sizeable impact on the way business was being done until the early 1970s, twenty-five years after the first working models were introduced. But from the first day the computer had some specific current applications, whether scientific calculation, making payroll or simulation to train pilots to fly airplanes... Unless there is an immediate application in the present, an innovation is like the drawings in Leonardo da Vinci's notebook – only a brilliant idea.

Source: Drucker (1985)

There are a number of tools you can use to help in a basic risk analysis of your ideas. To these tools should be added depth, in terms of the financial view from an accountant using financial tools.

Risk analysis

Risk analysis is a structured way of thinking through the problems associated with an innovation, development or change.

Working individually or as a team it should be possible to put together a list of all the barriers, risks and threats to the new idea.

Barriers or threats may be:

- human or time – related to the people in the organisation, their skills and the time they can devote to the innovation
- customer related – changes in society or to specific customer requirements
- operational or resource based – from disruption to supplies and operations
- reputational damage to reputation in the market
- procedural or policy related – from failures of internal systems and controls
- financial – from business failure, stock market, interest rates
- technical – new technology or technical failure
- environmental – threats from weather, natural disaster, accident, disease, etc.
- political – from changes in tax regimes, public opinion, government policy.

Involving others in this process is more likely to elicit objective judgments and different perspectives on the situation.

To construct a risk assessment matrix the process is:

1 identify the risks
2 assess the risks
3 produce responses to control or mitigate the risks
4 document the actions to be taken.

What are the risks?	*How important/ serious is the risk? 1 – low 5 – high*	*How likely is the risk? 1 – low 5 – high*	*Response to control or mitigate the risk*	*Actions*	*Risk rating = importance x likelihood*

Table 4.5 *Risk analysis matrix*

The higher the ultimate risk rating the more problematic the innovation is likely to be. Individually high risk factors need to be addressed as a matter of urgency.

Here is an example of a high-risk innovation risk assessment.

What are the risks?	*How important/ serious is the risk? 1 – low 5 – high*	*How likely is the risk? 1 – low 5 – high*	*Response to control or mitigate the risk*	*Actions*	*Risk rating = importance x likelihood*
The implementation will run over time and competitors will have an opportunity to steal market share.	5	3	Strict and tight implementation plan with the priority on getting the best version available on to the market on time.	Write contingency plan including must have features, nice to have and extras.	15
Organisational politics will put a stop to the new product development.	4	2	Networking and commitment raising.	Plan presentations to key stakeholders.	8
Lack of resources from suppliers will delay implementation.	3	2	Negotiate and gain realistic timescales from suppliers, and contingency plans.	Identify priority suppliers and negotiate contracts with suppliers. Create contingency plans.	6

Table 4.6 *Example risk analysis*

It is possible to see from this the level of planning and prioritising required. A full risk assessment should cover all or most of the potential barriers or threats using the following categories to help ensure that all angles are covered.

- Human or time related
- Customer related
- Operational, or resource based
- Reputational
- Procedural or policy related
- Financial
- Technical
- Environmental
- Political.

Cost benefit analysis

To calculate whether it's worth implementing an idea and the benefits you can expect you may need to complete a cost benefit analysis. This tool can be used to assess viability or risks and benefits.

Mindtools describes it like this.

> Cost Benefit Analysis or cba is a relatively simple and widely used technique for deciding whether to make a change. As its name suggests, to use the technique simply add up the value of the benefits of a course of action, and subtract the costs associated with it.
>
> Costs are either one-off, or may be ongoing. Benefits are most often received over time. We build this effect of time into our analysis by calculating a payback period. This is the time it takes for the benefits of a change to repay its costs. Many companies look for payback over a specified period of time – e.g. three years.

Source: www.mindtools.com/pages/article/newTED_08.htm

Cost benefit analysis can be used to analyse a change for which there are precedents. In other words, new products or services about which you have developed some experience. Or, less accurately, unprecedented or atypical change. Some argue that being too accurate may put anyone or any organisation in its right mind off radical change or development. Organisations that do attempt more sophisticated approaches to the justification of new developments usually base them on their experiences of difficulties of implementation. These might be unrelated areas. There is a lot of evidence to suggest that most organisations do not audit the results of their investment models.

An example of how a cost benefit analysis might be achieved in the NHS:

A team of people can produce a pretty adequate cost benefit analysis without the need to involve the financial experts in the organisation.

How to do it

1. Assemble the team.
2. Write a description of your proposal at the top of a flipchart.
3. Draw a vertical line down the middle of the flipchart.
4. At the top left hand column write 'Costs' and at the top right hand column write 'Benefits'.
5. Brainstorm for all of the costs involved in your solution. Only write up the descriptions of the costs, do not allocate any £s figures yet.
6. Brainstorm for all of the benefits involved in your solution. Only write up the descriptions of the benefits, do not allocate any £s figures yet.
7. Now go through each cost and benefit identified in the brainstorm and allocate the actual or estimated monetary value against each one. It pays to be conservative here. In other words, if you are not sure whether or not a particular cost will actually be involved, make the assumption that it will. If you are not sure whether or not a particular benefit will actually occur, make the assumption that it won't. If you are unsure of how much a cost will be, err on the high side. If you are unsure of how much a benefit will be, err on the low side. If you are conservative in this way and your analysis still shows an overall benefit, you can make your proposal with a high degree of confidence.
8. Add up all of the costs and add up all of the benefits.
9. Divide the total benefits by the total costs. If your proposal is going to deliver a payback, the answer needs to be greater than 1. Let's call the answer X. If X is less than 1 maybe you need to reconsider your proposal – except, of course when there are factors other than straight costs involved in your improvement proposal.
10. If X is greater than 1 your proposal can then take the form of, 'For every £ that we spend on this proposal we will receive £X'.

Figure 4.4 *How to conduct a cost benefit analysis*

Source: www.tin.nhs.uk/index.asp?pgid=1286 viewed October 2006

The cost benefit analysis is a simple tool that highlights some of the main issues with an idea. It also generates momentum around the idea and is part of the process of selling it internally.

Contingency planning

So what exactly could go wrong? Experience would suggest pretty much anything.

> **The most successful people are those who are good at Plan B.**
> **James Yorke**

Plan B arises typically out of the analyses that you have prepared in examining feasibility, viability and risk. Contingency planning is basically an extension of the risk assessment process. It typically involves a group of people with wide functional expertise putting their heads together to map out some likely scenarios and the proposed response to those scenarios

The trick is to raise the probability of success for the innovation through the planning process before the project begins. Contingency planning is about:

- time
- resources
- prioritising
- managing stakeholders.

Ensuring that people have enough time is essential. It may be possible to build in extra days, weeks, months or years at key points in the project to allow for catch up. This is an expensive option, but probably the most comfortable. Alternatively, you can put in more resources, suppliers, equipment, etc. into the project to make it happen on time. A less expensive option is effectively to modify your objectives by prioritising the 'must have' elements of the venture, using different technologies or methods or increasing flexibility. An element often missed in contingency planning is to manage the expectations of stakeholders. Keep them informed of progress. Surprises are far more uncomfortable than a project that is late or has taken a new direction, but which you were fully aware of. The other side of your relationship with your stakeholders is that they may be able to make suggestions, offer expertise or help you prioritise in a way that you could not have achieved yourself.

Activity 11
Risk analysis

Objective

Your objective is to carry out a cost benefit and risk analysis of a plan that you have in mind to implement. If you haven't used these tools before keep your plan simple. It's worth discussing both the cost benefit and risk analysis with your team.

Task

Write a description of your proposal.

Carry out a cost benefit analysis.

Cost benefit analysis

£	*Costs*	*Benefits*	*£*

Write a description of all the costs involved in your solution.

Write a description of all the benefits involved in your solution.

Now go through each cost and benefit identified and allocate the actual or estimated monetary value against each one.

Add up all of the costs and add up all of the benefits.

Divide the total benefits by the total costs. If your proposal is going to deliver a payback, the answer needs to be greater than 1. If X is greater than 1 your proposal can then take the form of, 'For every £ that we spend on this proposal we will receive £X'.

Risk analysis

Carry out a risk analysis of the same plan.

1. Identify the risks – the threats to your plan
2. Assess the risks
3. Produce responses to control or mitigate the risks
4. Document the actions to be taken.

What are the risks?	*How important/ serious is the risk? 1 – low 5 – high*	*How likely is the risk? 1 – low 5 – high*	*Response to control or mitigate the risk*	*Actions*	*Risk rating = importance x likelihood*

What conclusions can you draw about your plan from these two forms of analysis?

Feedback

These are only as good as the information you put in and can easily be skewed if that is your intention. They are, however, a useful and structured aid to decision making if used correctly and objectively. Most people in most organisations would be sceptical of a plan that appeared to have too many benefits or few risks.

One way of making them more objective is to show them to colleagues in your organisation. See what suggestions they can make. Another way to look at the benefits and risks is to imagine that it is your money that will go into the project (that is assuming that it isn't actually your money).

◆ Recap

'The best way to have a good idea is to have a lot of ideas.'

Dr Linus Pauling

True to the spirit of this Nobel prizewinning chemist and peace campaigner, this theme presents a multitude of ideas to help promote creativity and meaningful analysis of where you are now and where you want to go.

Use a variety of ways to generate creative solutions and make decisions

- The creative process around innovation rests on five planks of awareness:
  - *Value innovation* – how can you add value to your offer?
  - *Process innovation* – how can you improve processes?

- *Product innovation* – what products or services will our customers buy or use in the future?
- *Situational innovation* – how can we exploit an idea?
- *Technological innovation* – what technology can we exploit and how?

◆ Being aware of your environment and the competitive environment is fundamental to the creative process.

◆ Tools are listed and described to help you identify creative techniques and scan the organisational environment.

Use criteria to assess the feasibility and viability of new ideas

◆ Feasibility is the likelihood that your plan is possible to achieve, viability is the potential for the plan to be sustainable.

◆ There are a number of questions you need to ask to assess the feasibility of the plan. Is the opportunity consistent with the company's strategy? Will the factors that produced the opportunity last? What are the market characteristics? Is the opportunity worth the effort? Is the operation feasible – does the organisation have the skills, knowledge and experience in this market?

◆ The best advice from commentators is that you'll need to focus your idea and find out from the market or stakeholders what their opinions are. You should probably start small, doing one specific thing. And finally carry out a resource analysis to check the fit between what you do and what you are planning to do.

◆ Viability can be assessed using a range of financial and experiential tools, such as cash flow forecasting, analysis of the market volatility, experience of previous innovation, return on investment, net present value calculations, and payback periods.

◆ Force field analysis is proposed as a useful tool to help forestall difficulties and to support decision making.

Understand and evaluate the risks and benefits

◆ Risk analysis is a structured way of thinking through the problems associated with an innovation, development or change.

◆ Barriers or threats to your plan may be:

- human or time related
- customer related
- operational, or resource based
- reputational
- procedural or policy related
- financial
- technical
- environmental
- political.

- Benefits are normally measured in terms of currency values in a cost benefit analysis. This is not a precise tool, but a useful one for gaining an overall picture.

Build in contingency plans

Contingency planning is about:

- time
- resources
- prioritising
- managing stakeholders.

The following website is a useful source of tools for innovation. It forms the basis for the list of tools outlined in this section.

www.managing-innovation.com

Full references are provided at the end of the book.

References

Ansoff, I. (1957) Strategies for Diversification, *Harvard Business Review* (September-October)

Argyris, M. and Schön, D. (1974) *Theory in Practice: Increasing Professional Effectiveness*, San Francisco: Jossey-Bass

Argyris, C., and Schön, D. (1978) *Organisational Learning: A Theory of Action Perspective, Reading,* Mass: Addison Wesley.

Birley, S. and D. Muzyka (2000) *Mastering Entrepreneurship: The Complete MBA Companion in Entrepreneurship* FT Prentice Hall

Bygrave, W. D. (1997) *The Portable MBA in Entrepreneurship,* Wiley

de Bono, E. (1982) *Lateral Thinking for Management,* Penguin

Doole, I. and Lowe, R. (2005) Strategic Marketing Decisions in Global Markets, Thomson, London

Drucker, P. F. (1985) *Innovation and Entrepreneurship,* Elsevier Butterworth-Heinemann

Epstein, M. J., Shelton, R., Davila, R. (2005) *Making Innovation Work: How to Manage It, Measure It, and Profit from It,* Wharton School Publishing

Ettlie, J. E. (2006 2nd edition) *Managing Innovation,* Elsevier Butterworth-Heinemann

Johnson, G and Scholes, K (1999) *Exploring Corporate Strategy,* Prentice Hall Europe

Juran, J. M. (1951 1st edition) Quality Control Handbook, New York: McGraw-Hill.

Kaplan, R. S. and Norton, D. P. (1992) 'The balanced scorecard: measures that drive performance', *Harvard Business Review,* Jan – Feb pp71-80.

Kolb. D. A. and Fry, R. (1975) 'Toward an applied theory of experiential learning;, in C. Cooper (ed.) *Theories of Group Process,* London: John Wiley.

Lowe, R. and Marriot, S. (2006) *Enterprise: Entrepreneurship and Innovation,* Elsevier Butterworth-Heinemann

Lynch, R. (2000) *Corporate Strategy,* Financial Times, Prentice Hall

Mullins, L. J. (2002) *Management and Organisational Behaviour,* FT Prentice Hall

Mumford, M. D., and Porter, P. P. (1999) 'Analogies', in *Encyclopedia of Creativity,* (M.A.Runco, and S.R. Pritzker, eds.), Vol. 2, Academic Press, San Diego et al.:71-77

Porter, M. E. (1985) *Competitive Advantage,* The Free Press, New York

Tidd, J., Bessant, J. and Pavitt, K. (2001) *Managing Innovation,* John Wiley

Tidd, J., Bessant, J. and Pavitt, K. (2005) www.managing-innovation.com

Vadim Kotelnikov, adapted from Christopher Meyer, (1998) *Relentless Growth*, 1000 Ventures, www.1000ventures.com/business_guide/innovation_vs_operations.html

Watkins, M. (2003) *The first 90 days,* Harvard Business School Press

Websites

www.1000ventures.com/business_guide/innovation_vs_operations.html

www.barbaramintzer.com/newsletters/june2004.html

Business Week www.businessweek.com/magazine/content/06_25/b3989421.htm

Creativity & Innovation Library – Big and little innovation – www.jpb.com/creative/index.php

DTI Quality models www.dti.gov.uk/quality/qms

www.executive.modern.nhs.uk/framework/deliveringtheservice/collaborative.aspx

IBM, (2005) *Global Innovation Outlook – Innovation that Matters,* www.ibm.com

www.imaginatik.com/imaginatik/web.nsf/docs/idea_innovation

Leeds University www.leeds.ac.uk

www.managing-innovation.com

MOD www.contracts.mod.uk/dc/public/ebusiness/collaborative_working.htm

NHS Institute www.tin.nhs.uk/index.asp?pgid=1286 viewed October 2006

www.open2.net/money/innovation.html

QFD Institute www.qfdi.org/

Sainsbury www.sainsbury.co.uk

Time magazine www.time.com/time/magazine/article/0,9171,1187286,00.html Posted Sunday, Apr. 30, 2006

Virgin www.virgin.com

Wikipedia http://en.wikipedia.org/wiki/Net_present_value accessed October 2006